IDEA BANK

Creative Activities for the Language Class

Stephen A. Sadow
Northeastern University

NEWBURY HOUSE PUBLISHERS, INC.
ROWLEY, MASSACHUSETTS 01969
ROWLEY • LONDON • TOKYO
1 9 8 2

Library of Congress Cataloging in Publication Data

Sadow, Stephen A., 1946–
  Idea bank.

  1. English language--Study and teaching--
Foreign students. I. Title.
PE1128.A2S23 1982   418'.007   82–8247
ISBN 0-88377-218-3

Cover design by Leslie Bartlett

NEWBURY HOUSE PUBLISHERS, INC.

Language Science
Language Teaching
Language Learning

ROWLEY, MASSACHUSETTS 01969
ROWLEY • LONDON • TOKYO

First printing: October 1982

Printed in the U.S.A.

5   4   3

For Alex Lipson

ACKNOWLEDGMENTS

A lot of great teachers/friends helped in the making of this book. Most are professional language teachers; a few are in other pursuits. All want teaching to be all that it can be. Moreover, they were there when I needed them. First, I want to thank George Reeves who got me started on the project. Many others deserve my thanks. Greatly appreciated, they are: Anne Dow, Holbrook Robinson, Sandee Leftoff, Bill Biddle, Ross Hall, Jeff Kaplan, Steve Molinsky, Lynn Stevens, Cindy Lawrence, Monica Maxwell, Dan Barker, Bill Sypher, Laurie Greller, Ellen Rintell, Gladys Varona-Lacey, Ray Comeau, Juliette Gilman, Cathy Cogen, Dorothy Bullimore, Ellen Crocker, Linda Tuttle, Leslie Kagan, Melanie Schneider, Malka Lifshitz, Laurie Feldman, Joan Perkins, and Marta Rosso-O'Laughlin. I hope I didn't miss anyone.

I'd also like to thank my students of Spanish at Northeastern University and of ESL at Harvard Summer School for their good humor, willingness to participate in my schemes, and their often amazing creativity.

Finally, Elizabeth Lantz of Newbury House deserves a round of applause for her support, perceptive comments, good advice, and patience.

TABLE OF CONTENTS

Impersonate—*Act it out!*

Appendices

IDEA BANK

INTRODUCTION

There are times in the life of every language teacher when ideas seem to have run out. Students follow along, making drill transformations or trying to unscramble the plot of a literary text, but a sense of excitement is missing. The goals remain the same: students are to use newly acquired skills to express themselves in speech and in writing (or in sign). Yet free conversations flounder and last year's composition themes fail to interest this year's students.

The activities in this book were conceived as a response to language class doldrums. They are intended to change the pace, to break the routine. However, the activities are definitely not time killers. All of them stimulate students to practice communicative skills; emphasis is on skill-using rather than skill-getting. Through a variety of strategies, the activities provoke students to what Earl Stevick would call "productivity"[1] and what Wilga Rivers labels "autonomous interaction."[2] These activities provide students with problems they are interested in solving and create a supportive non-threatening situation in which they are likely to solve them.

These activities are intended for use in any language class, regardless of the language being taught. While especially appropriate to college- and high school-level courses, many of them can be adapted for use with children. They have been tested in Spanish, French, German, Hebrew, and American Sign Language classes as well as ESL classes. Easily, they can be adapted to Italian, Japanese, Arabic, or any other spoken or signed language. For teachers of ESL, Spanish, French, and German (the most commonly taught languages in the United States), special appendices provide translations of the key section of each lesson and also lists of suggested vocabulary.

There are four types of activities. In the *Mind bending* group, students are asked to identify and explain something which is inherently ambiguous; in *Brainstorm,* they must devise a plan or an invention; in *Sell–Sell–Sell,* they produce advertising copy; and in *Impersonate,* they act out specific roles. But while their orientation and content vary greatly, all forty-five activities share underlying characteristics. First, they are task-oriented. Problems must be solved or roles acted out within a limited time span. Second, they are done in a non-threatening atmosphere. Many activities call for small groups of students working together without teacher interference. Third, role-play is used throughout. Each activity calls for the students' taking on new guises. This technique allows them to step out of themselves and away from their usual concerns. In many cases, the

---

[1]Earl Stevick. *Memory, Meaning and Method.* Rowley, Mass.: Newbury House (1976), pp. 116–19.

[2]Wilga Rivers. *Speaking in Many Tongues: Essays in Foreign Language Teaching.* Rowley, Mass.: Newbury House (1976), p. 23.

role-play flatters the students by making them experts and giving them identities which are held in high esteem. This role-play allows a great deal of fantasy to come forth. Fourth, the activities are, in fact, creativity exercises. Students are challenged to produce new answers and new combinations. All coherent solutions are applauded. Students can be practical, fanciful, or both, in their responses. Playfulness is encouraged. Fifth, skill-using predominates. Students *listen* to (or *watch* the signing of) a story and instructions. They *discuss* possible solutions. They *practice* new vocabulary and *review* grammatical structures. They *write* down their conclusions and *read* them to the class. Sixth, the activities are self-contained exercises which can be introduced into a course at any point. They can be tied to a particular unit or employed independently. A single one, or all forty-five, can be used during a single course. Finally, the activities are not tied to any one culture. They could take place in many. In some cases, the situation presented—paying tuition, for example—may not occur in the target culture. This should not preclude the activity's use as a communicative exercise. Students can simply be told that the situation "couldn't really happen in Germany." Conversely, many of the activities lead quite naturally to cultural or cross-cultural discussions.

How to use the activities

Directions for each activity are presented in a lesson plan format. With some minor variations, each lesson plan will include the same sections listed in the same order. Keep in mind that these plans are intended to be taken as suggestions rather than rigid recipe-like injunctions. Depending on the nature of your class and your own personal style, you should feel free to modify or even eliminate steps.

The sections consist of:

Objectives While all the activities share the same general objectives of stimulating language production and creative thinking, the specific purposes vary widely. Some activities call for the use of certain grammatical forms—the imperatives, for example—while others emphasize concepts such as weights and measures. Practical thinking about social problems is called for, as are flights of pure fantasy. In each activity a list of specific objectives is given. You can use these to help you decide when to employ a particular activity.

Prepare Many of the activities can be done without any props or extra materials. Some, like those in the "Mind bending" category, require that you bring something to class. Other activities can be enhanced with a few easily obtainable props. If a prop is necessary or would help, you are told what to bring, or how to prepare a facsimile.

2

Tell the class You announce to the class that a problem exists. For each activity, there is a script relating the nature of the particular situation. The script is a model. Use it as is or adjust the vocabulary and any specific references to your classes' linguistic abilities and sophistication. If you are a teacher of languages other than English, when translating, you may have to make small adjustments to account for linguistic and cultural constraints inherent in those languages (forms of address, for example). Translations of the scripts into French, Spanish, and German are found in the appendices.

Most of the scripts are intended to be humorous; some are more serious. The humorous scripts should be presented with a mock severity. By the use of an exaggerated tone of voice, you can signal to the class the "tongue in cheek" nature of what you are saying. The activities work best when an element of fun is introduced. The way you present the script will affect the mood in which the activities are undertaken.

Check comprehension The scripts are, in effect, listening comprehension exercises. While presenting the story, stop occasionally. In lower class levels, repeat it more than once. Ask a few short questions to test for comprehension, such as; "Where was I last night?"; "What happened to me?"; "What is the problem?"; "Why has this class been asked to solve it?"

Present vocabulary; Reinforce grammar Space has been provided for you to jot down vocabulary which you think will help your students do the activity. In the appendices, you will find relevant vocabulary of varying difficulty in English, French, Spanish, and German. It is provided solely as a stimulus. Freely substitute other words that come to mind. Limit the number of words taught or reviewed; presenting more than ten words breaks up the flow of the activity. Advanced classes may need only a word or two.

You may want to begin the vocabulary section with a statement like: "Before you get to work on the project, let's go over some words you may want to use."

Some of the activities will be more effective if certain grammar points are reinforced. Do not teach grammar here but instead remind students of forms they will need: "Let's practice some forms that you'll need when you talk about this problem."

Ask the class Before the students work on the problem, they should have a clear idea of what questions they need to respond to. A list of questions will help guide their thinking and give them linguistic models for their utterances. You can elicit questions from the class and supplement these with others you want them to answer. A set of sample questions is provided. Some of the questions can be used as a means of eliciting grammatical structures. For example, you ask a question in an imperfect tense and call for an answer employing the same tense. The questions should be written on the board; sample answers should not, for they could inhibit other responses.

Divide the class The majority of the activities employ small groups of three to five students. Others call for students to work singly, in pairs, or with the whole class. For each activity there is a suggested group size. You may experiment with different combinations, but keep in mind that in groups of more than five there is less intimacy and less likelihood that shier students will participate.

There are many ways of dividing students into groups.[3] Use whatever method has worked for you in other situations. The quickest is to simply count off students into groups of the desired numbers. In some of the activities there are three or more problems being treated. You may ask for volunteers to work on the theme they prefer. Don't let the same students work together all the time.

Have the groups choose a secretary; do not appoint one. The secretary will later report to the class what was decided. It is the secretary's task to take notes on what is being discussed or in some cases to write down advertising as it is being formulated. They should write as grammatically as they can, but the emphasis should be on recording what is said rather than accuracy of form.

The device of having a secretary acts as a control on the group and keeps it from getting sidetracked. The knowledge that they will have to report to the class makes it less likely that they will waste their time.

Do the activity Remind the class of the questions on the blackboard. You may tell them to discuss the problem freely and prepare their report. In lower-level classes or in classes where students are hesitant to participate, a more rigorous strategy may be invoked. Tell the groups that each student is to suggest an answer to each question. The group should then decide which answer they like the best and have their secretary record it. In full class, single, or paired activities, the secretary device is not employed.

Call for reports When enough time has elapsed, ask the secretary or individuals (if the activity has been a writing exercise) to read their conclusions aloud to the class. The comparing of results greatly adds to the students' enjoyment and sense of accomplishment.

In-class discussion topics While the activities in this book are intended to be self-contained, you may want to expand upon them by preceding or following them with a class discussion of relevant issues. A list of possible topics is given in each lesson plan.

Follow-up writing topics You may want to reinforce the class work with a writing assignment to be done outside of class. This writing may be of an expository nature—short paragraphs or essays—or could include dialogues,

---

[3]See Gertrude Moskowitz. *Caring and Sharing in the Foreign Language Class.* Rowley, Mass.: Newbury House (1978), pp. 36–8.

4

narrative fiction, short plays, alternative answers to the problems discussed in class, or anything else you deem appropriate. Sample themes are provided.

More directions

Timing of activities The exact amount of time spent on any activity will depend on your class. Twenty-five minutes is sufficient for any of the activities. Do not plan less than fifteen minutes.

Frequency of use While not absolutely necessary, an element of surprise can add to the excitement of the activities. Do not announce them beforehand. They are meant to be changes of pace. Doing about one per week would accustom the class to the type of necessary interactions while maintaining interest in the problems. Some activities are better the second or third time they are tried with a particular class.

Correction Monitor the groups to watch for student participation. Correct very sparingly if at all. Do nothing that would inhibit students from speaking voluntarily. When the secretaries give their reports, correct only the most glaring errors.

Use of languages other than the target language Follow your normal practice as to how much speech in languages other than the target language you permit. You may want to act as a "walking dictionary," reacting to "How do you say _____ ?" Out of frustration, students may lapse into their native language from time to time. Remind them to use the language being studied. Most likely, this problem will decrease as students become accustomed to the activities.

Use of scripts as writing assignments Any of the activity scripts can be easily transformed into a writing assignment. Simply give the students a handout with a problem written out in script form. You may want to add some vocabulary. Correct in your normal manner. The activities could form the basis for the writing segment of a course.

Advanced classes In advanced classes, it may be sufficient to tell students the problem, divide them into groups, and allow them to proceed.

Creation of your own activities The activities in this book fall into four basic categories which have proved successful. They do not begin to exhaust the possibilities. Once you are familiar with the general format, invent your own versions.

What to expect Students often come up with responses which are extraordinarily creative. You will be amazed at their inventiveness. Occasionally it does occur, however, that a particular group or class proposes rather mundane answers. Do not be dismayed. The primary objective is to promote use of the language. As long as students talk, the activity is a success. If a group seems stuck, you may offer a suggestion or two, but don't interfere. Their solutions must be their own.

One last instruction about the use of this book: Enjoy it!

Levels of the activities

This section is intended to help you select the activities appropriate to the language level of your class. Consider it a guide rather than an injunction. Some activities are directly applicable at all levels. Many others can be adjusted upward or downward by changing the vocabulary used or practicing structures. Do not be afraid to try any activity your class can handle. Moreover, advanced classes often have great success developing simpler topics.

"Beginning" level is used to refer to the latter part of the first year of high school or of the first-semester college language courses, "Intermediate" to second- or third-year high school courses and second- or third-semester college courses, and "Advanced" to fourth-year high school courses and fourth-semester college courses and beyond. Teachers in other sorts of situations will have to judge for themselves, but can use these divisions as a rough guide.

All levels

Treasures	Flim-flam	Taxi driver
Family portrait	Quick sale	Tour guide
Omelet		

Beginning–Intermediate

Flagging	Soft soap	Visiting scholar
Perfect person		

Intermediate–Advanced

Art critic	Student center	Alma mater
Flute flight	House party	Campaign
Tapestry	Hobby town	Tourist office
College application	Chef	Mansion
Character sketch	Floating	Air waves
Recycle	Toyland	Last rites
Dinner party	Snake oil	Nostalgia
Vacation	Planning board	High society
Animal house	Used car	

Advanced

Shipwreck
Zodiac
Tribal council

Dead language
Visitation
Honored guest

Convention
Emergency

Thematic guide to the activities

Some teachers will want to coordinate the activities with other material being presented to the class. The tie-in works best when done thematically. Use this section as a guide. But, in all cases, make sure that the language level of the activity is appropriate to your class.

Theme

Activities

Theme	Activities
Animals	Animal house
Art	Art critic
Automobiles	Used car
Buildings	House party, Mansion
Colors	Art critic, Tapestry, Flagging
Describing people	Family portrait, College application, Character sketch, Perfect person, Zodiac, Campaign, Last rites
Describing places	Vacation, Tourist office, Taxi driver, Tour guide
Describing things	Treasures, Tapestry, Flagging, Floating, Recycle, Quick sale, Soft soap
Emergencies	Shipwreck, Tribal council, Emergency
Food	Omelet, Dinner party, Chef
Hobbies and games	Hobby town, Toyland
Languages	Dead language
Medicine	Snake oil
Meeting people	Taxi driver, Visiting scholar, High society, Visitation, Convention
Money	Flim-flam, Quick sale
Music	Flute flight
Politics	Planning board, Campaign, Honored guest
Radio	Air waves
School and college	Student center, Alma mater, Nostalgia

THE ACTIVITIES

Mind bending—*What is it?*

Treasures—*What could it be?*

Objectives

To practice describing objects
To establish the value of something
To use descriptive adjectives

Prepare   Select an object that will not be readily identifiable by students. Knickknacks and figurines from faraway places or unusual kitchen gadgets work well. The exact nature of the object is not as important as its being ambiguous and subject to various interpretations.

Tell the class

I'm very puzzled. This morning on the way to school, I was stopped by a man carrying a large paper bag. He took *this* object from the bag. He assured me that it was of great value, but since he needed the money he would sell it to me for only $100. I can never pass up a bargain, so I bought it immediately. Now I'm not so sure I did well since I have no idea what this thing is. I know all of you are experts in antiques, so I'm asking you to explain this thing to me and tell me whether I have been cheated.*

Check comprehension

Present vocabulary

*In this and all subsequent activities, a footnote will direct you to the Spanish, French, and German translations of the *Tell the class* sections and to the vocabulary lists for these languages and English given in the appendices. For English, see page 103; for Spanish, see page 108; for French, see page 123; for German, see page 137.

Ask the class   What questions will you need to answer? (Write the questions on the blackboard.)

1. What is it?
2. How old is it?
3. What does it do?
4. What color is it? What shape?
5. What does it resemble?
6. Is there a story behind it?
7. Is it valuable? Very valuable?
8. Was the teacher cheated?
9. If it were mine, what would I do with it?

Divide the class   Form groups of three to five students each. Have each group choose a secretary. Remind them of the questions on the blackboard.

Do the activity

Call for reports   The secretaries read the conclusions. Encourage other students to ask questions and make comments. Summarize the responses.

In-class discussion topics

1. How do we know a bargain?
2. How do we test for quality?
3. Why are antiques and old things important to us?
4. What are the artifacts of the present?

Follow-up writing topics

1. My greatest bargain
2. The time I was cheated
3. Collecting as a pastime
4. The uses of decorative art

Use this space for writing in vocabulary

11

Family portrait—*I never would have recognized you*

Objectives

To describe people and personal relationships
To invent life stories
To practice using descriptive adjectives

Prepare   Select a photograph of a group of people. The photograph should contain at least four people and should look like it is at least fifty years old. Old family photographs or pictures of Old West outlaws or of early aviators work well. The photograph should be big enough for it to be seen when held up in front of the class.

Tell the class

Last night I was up in my attic and I happened to open an old steamer trunk that was covered with dust. In the trunk I found this photograph. There are no markings on it, but I suspect that I'm related to some of the people in the picture. I know you are all experts in family history. I just couldn't wait to show you the picture so that you could tell me who these people were and what they were doing just before the photograph was taken.*

Check comprehension

Present vocabulary

Ask the class   What questions will you ask about this picture? (Write the questions on the blackboard.)

1. Who are these people?
2. How are they dressed?
3. Are they related to each other?
4. What are they doing?
5. Why did they have their picture taken? Who was the photographer?
6. Where are they?
7. Are they related to the teacher?

*For English, see page 103; for Spanish, page 108; for French, page 123; for German, page 137.

Divide the class   Form groups of three to five students each. Have each group choose a secretary. Remind them of the questions on the blackboard.

Do the activity

Call for reports   The secretaries read their conclusions. Encourage other students to ask questions and make comments. Summarize the responses.

In-class discussion topics
1. Why are people interested in family history?
2. Why are group portraits taken?
3. How can photographs distort the truth?
4. What will your grandchildren say about photographs of you?

Follow-up writing topics
1. My most famous relative; my favorite relative
2. Searching for my family history
3. Making a photo history
4. My ties to the past

Use this space for writing in vocabulary

Art critic—*It's a masterpiece!*

Objectives

To practice looking carefully at a work of art
To describe the contents of a picture
To encourage students to make up stories about what they see

Prepare   Select a number of reproductions of art works done in abstract or primitive styles. There should be one picture for every five students in the class. Postcard-size reproductions work well; art books clipped open to specific pages can also serve.

Tell the class

As some of you may know, my dear uncle Oscar was an art collector famous for the strange and unusual works in his collection. He used to say that in each work of art there is hidden a story. Well, uncle Oscar died last month and left to me some of his favorite pieces. The trouble is that I just don't know anything about art, and I just can't figure out what the pictures mean or why they are valuable. Since I know that you are all experts in art interpretation and art history, I'm asking you to tell the stories shown in these works and evaluate their importance.*

Check comprehension

Present vocabulary

Ask the class   What questions will you need to answer as you study the pictures? (Write the questions on the blackboard.)

1. Where does it take place?
2. Are there people in the picture? Who are they?
3. Are there animals in the picture?
4. What colors are most important?
5. What is happening?
6. What story does the picture tell?
7. What can we tell about the artist?
8. Is the painting valuable? Why or why not?

*For English, see page 103; for Spanish, page 108; for French, page 123; for German, page 137.

Divide the class   Form groups of three to five students each. Where it is practical to do so, allow the students to choose the picture they want to discuss. Otherwise, divide them arbitrarily. Have each group choose a secretary. Remind them of the questions on the blackboard.

Do the activity

Call for reports   The secretaries read the stories their groups have made up and comment on the painting's value. Encourage other students to ask questions and make comments.

In-class discussion topics

1. What is the purpose of abstract art?
2. Why do people collect art?
3. Why is some art popular while other art is not?
4. Do art works really tell stories?
5. Should all great works of art be in public museums? Why?

Follow-up writing topics

1. My favorite artist
2. The problems of the young artist
3. Current exhibitions at local museums

Use this space for writing in vocabulary

Flute flight—*Whistle a happy tune*

Objectives

To listen carefully to an unfamiliar piece of music
To stimulate interpretation and appreciation of music
To practice vocabulary relating to music and sound

Prepare   Select a record or tape of a piece of unusual or exotic music. The work should last about three minutes. Pick a piece that you believe will be new to the students. Depending on your group, South American, African, or Oriental folk music could be used. Little-known classical music is also appropriate. Choose instrumental music; avoid distracting lyrics. Bring a tape recorder or record player to class and test it before class starts.

Tell the class

Last summer when I was traveling in a faraway country, I heard music which was unlike any I had ever listened to before. Its special qualities intrigued me. To my good fortune, I was able to purchase a recording of it. Being in a hurry, I didn't have time to inquire about the origins and meaning of this music. I do remember hearing, however, that the people of that region often used music to tell stories. All of you are experts about the music of the world, so I'm asking you to figure out the origins of this music and retell its story.*

Check comprehension

Present vocabulary

Ask the class   What questions will you need to ask about the music? (Write the questions on the blackboard.)

1. What is the mood?
2. Is it happy or sad?
3. What does it make you think of?
4. Where was it recorded?
5. What story is being told?

*For English, see page 103; for Spanish, page 109; for French, page 124; for German, page 138.

Divide the class   Form groups of three to five students each. Have each group choose a secretary. Remind them of the questions on the blackboard.

Do the activity   Ask for complete silence. Play the piece of music twice.

Call for reports   The secretaries read the stories. Encourage other students to ask questions and make comments.

In-class discussion topics

1. Why is some music more popular than other music?
2. Do composers really tell stories through their music?
3. Why do people spend endless hours learning to play instruments? Is it worth it?
4. Why do some people dislike classical music while others dislike popular music?

Follow-up writing topics

1. Music in today's society
2. My favorite composer; my favorite piece of music
3. Learning to play an instrument
4. Inventing a new musical instrument

Use this space for writing in vocabulary

Tapestry—*Silver threads among the gold*

Objectives

To see a simple piece of cloth in many different ways
To practice vocabulary related to cloth and clothing

Prepare   Select a piece of multi-colored fabric with a repeating design, about three feet by two feet in size. If possible, the fabric should be hand-woven.

Tell the class

I have with me today a very unusual piece of cloth. It was made according to a secret process by weavers who died long ago. As far as I know, this is the last piece left. This cloth is extremely useful and has many wondrous qualities. I'm glad you are all here today. Those of you who are textile manufacturers will have the opportunity to devise a process for reproducing the material; those who sell textiles can list the possible uses of this cloth; those of you who are experts in world religions can explain the religious system symbolized by the repeating patterns in the fabric.*

Check comprehension

Present vocabulary

Ask the class   What questions do we need to ask about this cloth? (Write the questions on the blackboard.)

1. How can we find out what the cloth is made of?
2. How can we make it now?
3. What do we need in order to make it?
4. What can the cloth be used for?
5. What unusual qualities does it have?
6. How is it different?
7. What is the meaning of the pattern?
8. What do the colors stand for?
9. Why do the patterns repeat?

*For English, see page 103; for Spanish, page 109; for French, page 124; for German, page 138.

Divide the class   Assign an equal number of students to each of the projects: how to reproduce the fabric, how to use the fabric, what the symbols mean. Form groups of three to five students each. Have each group choose a secretary. Remind them of the questions on the blackboard. Tell them that not all of the questions are relevant to their problem.

Do the activity

Call for reports   The secretaries read their reports. Encourage other students to ask questions and make comments. Summarize the reports.

In-class discussion topics

1. How can ancient methods be useful today?
2. What are the advantages of mass production?
3. Why are some colors and patterns so popular?
4. How has cloth changed in recent years?

Follow-up writing topics

1. Making your own clothes
2. Religious symbols
3. Bringing back old skills

Use this space for writing in vocabulary

College application—*Who is it?*

Objectives

To create fanciful life stories
To assemble personal data
To use persuasive language

Prepare   Select a picture of a mermaid, centaur, or other man-beast. These can be found in illustrated books of mythology or folklore. The picture should be big enough to be visible to the whole class.

Tell the class

The secretary of the admissions committee of Heckster College just called. They received a highly unusual application and don't know what to do about it. They want to be fair to the applicant, but they have never seen anyone like him (or her). To make matters worse, someone spilled coffee on the application and now much of it is illegible. Since there isn't sufficient time in which to contact the applicant, the admissions committee needs your help. They are asking you, as experts in other cultures, to figure out what the application must have said. They need to know who he (or she) is and why he (or she) thinks he (or she) should be admitted. Here is the picture that was attached to the application. (Show the picture.)*

Variation   If appropriate, the name of the college could be changed to the school or program in which the students are enrolled.

Check comprehension

Present vocabulary

Ask the class   What do we have to answer about the applicant? (Write the questions on the blackboard.)

1. Who is it? What is his (or her) name?
2. Where is he (or she) from?
3. What education has the applicant had?
4. What are the applicant's special talents and abilities?
5. Why does the applicant want to study at this college?

*For English, see page 103; for Spanish, page 109; for French, page 124; for German, page 138.

Divide the class   Form groups of three to five students each. Have each group choose a secretary. Remind them of the questions on the blackboard.

Do the activity

Call for reports   The secretaries read the applications their groups have prepared. Encourage other students to ask questions and make comments.

In-class discussion topics

1. Why go to college, anyway?
2. Who should go to college?
3. Are admissions decisions fair?
4. What are the responsibilities of the admissions committee?

Follow-up writing topics

1. Getting into college
2. Open admissions
3. Planning for higher education
4. Going away to school or college

Use this space for writing in vocabulary

Character sketch—*Looks familiar*

Objectives

To help students visualize what they are reading
To enforce careful reading of descriptive material
To practice descriptive adjectives associated with people

Prepare   This activity works best when done in conjunction with readings which are already part of the coursework. Select three to five sections from the reader in which real or fictitious people are described. The selections should cover physical appearance as well as personality traits. They should not be more than one page in length. For an advanced class, the selections could be new to the students. Otherwise, they should be sections with which the students are familiar so that vocabulary will not be a problem.

Bring blank paper to class.

Tell the class

The editor of these texts has decided that there must be illustrations in the next edition. This editor believes that having pictures of the main characters will help sell more books. Since all of you are well-known artists, you've received a contract to do the drawings. Remember, your work should picture exactly what you read.*

Check comprehension

Check vocabulary   Review vocabulary from the selections.

Ask the class   What questions will you have to ask before you start to draw? (Write the questions on the blackboard.)

1. Who is it?
2. What does he or she look like? Tall? Short? Fat? Thin?
3. What is this person's most important characteristic?
4. When did this person live?
5. What is this person wearing?

*For Spanish translation, see page 110; for French, page 125; for German, page 139. There are no vocabulary lists for this activity.

Divide the class   Tell the students to choose the person that they would most like to draw. This activity can be done as an individual project with students working alone. Or, form groups of three to five students each. Pass out the drawing paper. Tell them to collaborate in producing one drawing. It is not important that an equal number of students work on each selection. As far as is practical, allow them to work on their favorite. Remind them of the questions on the blackboard.

Do the activity   The individuals or groups draw their illustrations.

Call for reports   Each student or group shows a drawing to the class. They explain what they have done. Encourage other students to ask questions and make comments.

In-class discussion topics

1. What is the value of having illustrations in books?
2. How do authors describe people?
3. Why do some people prefer comic books to regular books?
4. Does one picture equal one thousand words?

Follow-up writing topics

1. A picture is worth a thousand words—or is it?
2. Illustrating children's books
3. Making books and magazines that are attractive
4. My favorite illustrations

Use this space for writing in vocabulary

Brainstorm—*What can we do with it?*

Omelet—*Scramble*

Objectives

To practice dealing with an urgent problem
To practice food and cooking vocabulary

Prepare   No props are required for this activity.

Tell the class

We've got a problem! There has been a computer error. Tomorrow, at this time, one million eggs will be delivered to this classroom. It would be a terrible waste to let the eggs spoil. Since you are experts in food use and distribution, you should plan as many ways as possible to use and distribute the eggs.*

Check comprehension

Present vocabulary

Ask the class   What questions will you ask about the eggs? (Write the questions on the blackboard.)

1. Where can we put the eggs?
2. Where can we send the eggs?
3. How can we use the eggs?
4. How long will it be before the eggs spoil?

*For English, see page 103; for Spanish, page 110; for French, page 125; for German, page 139.

Divide the class Form groups of three to five students each. Have the groups choose a secretary. Tell them to make lists of uses and methods of distribution. Remind them of the questions on the blackboard.

Do the activity

Call for reports The secretaries read their lists. Summarize the lists on the blackboard.

In-class discussion topics

1. How can we waste less food?
2. How can countries use surplus food?
3. Do countries with a good food supply have an obligation to poorer countries? Why or why not?

Follow-up writing topics

1. Eating well
2. Cooking creatively
3. Better ways to distribute food throughout the world
4. Consumer food cooperatives and other ways of saving money by buying food in quantity

---

Use this space for writing in vocabulary

Flim-flam—*Never give a sucker an even break!*

Objectives

To consider unusual ways of making money
To play at being slightly dishonest
To practice talking about money

Prepare   No props are required for this activity.

Tell the class

I'm broke! I just can't make ends meet on a teacher's (professor's) salary. You know how little teachers are paid. What I need is a "get rich quick" scheme. Since I know that you are specialists in making money, but are not, shall we say, absolutely honest, I thought that you could suggest a way for me to make a lot of money in a short period of time. Fooling the public is definitely O.K., but be careful. I don't want to go to jail.*

Check comprehension

Present vocabulary

Ask the class   What must you ask about the "get rich quick" scheme? (Write the questions on the blackboard.)

1. What should the teacher do?
2. What costume is necessary?
3. How much will the teacher need to spend?
4. Is the plan dishonest or illegal? How?
5. What vehicles or other things are necessary?

*For English, see page 103; for Spanish, page 110; for French, page 125; for German, page 139.

Divide the class   Form groups of three to five students each. You may want to give the groups fanciful names like "The Gang of Five" or the "Mississippi Mob." Have the groups choose a secretary. Remind them of the questions on the blackboard.

Do the activity

Call for reports   The secretaries read the schemes. Pretend to be shocked by them. Encourage the other students to react.

In-class discussion topics
1. Were you ever cheated?
2. What is the quickest way to get rich?
3. What are some of the most famous schemes for cheating the public?
4. Is cheating ever acceptable? Why or why not?
5. How can you protect yourself against dishonest business practices?

Follow-up writing topics
1. Protecting yourself against the unscrupulous
2. Honesty in business
3. Cheating
4. Famous frauds and swindles

Use this space for writing in vocabulary

Flagging—*Long may it wave*

Objectives

To consider the relationship between symbols and meaning
To practice vocabulary of colors, shapes, and patterns

Prepare   While this activity can be done without props, you may want to bring a pad of blank paper and colored crayons to class.

Tell the class

Hooray! Long live the Republic of Bartonia! Bartonia has just been granted its independence. There is dancing in the streets! There is one problem, however. Bartonia's founders have not been able to agree on a flag for the new state. The ambassador asks you, expert flag makers, to design a flag. The colors and patterns that you choose should have great meaning for the citizens of Bartonia.

If there is time, you can also compose a pledge of allegiance to the flag.*

Check comprehension

Present vocabulary

Ask the class   What questions do flag makers ask? (Write the questions on the blackboard.)

1. How big will the flag be?
2. What colors will it have?
3. What do these colors stand for?
4. What will the flag look like?
5. Will there be any symbols on it?

*For English, see page 103; for Spanish, page 111; for French, page 125; for German, page 139.

Divide the class   Form groups of three to five students each. If you wish, pass out drawing paper to the groups and make crayons available. Remind them of the questions on the blackboard.

Do the activity

Call for reports   The groups present their flag designs. They explain the meaning of the colors and patterns they have chosen. Encourage students to ask questions and make comments.

In-class discussion topics

1. Why do countries have flags? What purpose do they serve?
2. Why are there so many ceremonies relating to flags?
3. What kinds of flags are used? When?
4. Which countries have the most beautiful flags?

Follow-up writing topics

1. The significance of national flags
2. Famous flags
3. Flag-raising ceremonies
4. Unusual types of flags

Use this space for writing in vocabulary

Perfect person—*My hero!*

Objectives

To consider positive qualities of people
To practice describing people
To practice vocabulary related to character traits and physical characteristics

Prepare   No props are required for this activity.

Tell the class

It bothers me a lot that every single person I meet is imperfect! I'm really
tired of it! Everyone I know has faults, weaknesses, bad habits, and other
imperfections. I'm asking you, as biologists, to design the *perfect person.**

Check comprehension

Present vocabulary

Ask the class   What questions do you need to ask about a perfect person?
(Write the questions on the blackboard.)

1. What does this person look like?
2. What type of personality does this person have? How can we describe this
   personality?
3. What makes this person special?
4. What sort of work does this person do?
5. What has this person achieved?

*For English, see page 104; for Spanish, page 111; for French, page 126; for German, page 140.

Divide the class   Form groups of three to five students each. Have the groups choose a secretary. Remind them of the questions on the blackboard.

Do the activity

Call for reports   The secretaries read the descriptions to the class. Ask the other students if they agree that this person is indeed perfect. Summarize the descriptions.

In-class discussion topics

1.   What makes a person admirable?
2.   Why do some people become national heroes?
3.   What are the best qualities a person can have?
4.   If you met a "perfect person," would you like him or her?

Follow-up writing topics

1.   My ideal person
2.   My favorite person; my hero
3.   Building character
4.   The type of person I want to be

Use this space for writing in vocabulary

Recycle—*New lamps for old*

Objectives

To see familiar objects in new ways
To stimulate rapid thinking

Prepare   Write on the blackboard a list of objects that are normally discarded or returned after they are used or worn out. The list may include things like tires, glass bottles, auto batteries, light bulbs, and shoes. Try to include two or three more unusual items like stereo sets, refrigerators, and butterfly nets.

Tell the class

There is just too much waste! The local dump is filled with things that could be used again. The mayor has asked you, experts in recycling, to make up lists of new uses for old things.*

Variation   Limit the discussion to parts of old cars.

Check comprehension

Present vocabulary

Ask the class   What questions do we ask about an old thing? (Write the questions on the blackboard.)

1. What does it do?
2. What else could it do?
3. How could it be changed or adapted?

*For English, see page 104; for Spanish, page 111; for French, page 126; for German, page 140.

Divide the class   This activity works well with groups of two, three or four students each. Have the pairs or groups choose a secretary. Remind them of the questions on the blackboard. This activity can also be done in a whole-class, teacher-directed fashion.

Do the activity   Tell the groups to discuss the objects one at a time. Each group should appoint a secretary to record the lists. They should write down as many new uses for each object as they can think of. When they get stuck, they should move on to the next object. Set a time limit of twenty minutes.

If you prefer to do an all-class activity, elicit new uses from the class and write them on the blackboard. When there is a lull, move to the next object.

Call for reports   Have the secretaries read their lists. Let each group report on a different object. Summarize the class's responses on the blackboard.

In-class discussion topics

1. Is recycling worth the time and effort it entails?
2. Why is so much thrown away?
3. Should all areas have recycling programs?
4. What are the advantages and disadvantages of buying used merchandise?

Follow-up writing topics

1. An effective recycling program
2. The many uses of "junk "
3. What to look for when buying a used car, used furniture, or used clothing
4. Totally new uses for worn-out things

Use this space for writing in vocabulary

Dinner party—*They'll be here soon*

Objectives

To plan a meal
To practice using food vocabulary
To practice weights and measures

Prepare   Collect beforehand copies of newspaper supermarket ads in the language being studied (one for every five students is sufficient). Teachers of Spanish and ESL will find these easy to obtain. Teachers of other languages will have to search; if necessary, a facsimile can be made up and copied.

Tell the class

I hope you didn't forget that there will be six people coming for dinner at your house (or dormitory) tomorrow night. Since there isn't much time, it would help a great deal if you could choose the menu based on what one store is selling. Fortunately, they advertise in the language we've been studying. Using the information in the ad, plan a delicious meal. You can spend as much as you want, but record your expenses.*

Check comprehension

Present vocabulary   Familiarize students with units of weights and measures.

Ask the class   What questions do you have to keep in mind when planning a menu? (Write the questions on the blackboard.)

1. What do my guests and I like?
2. What is available?
3. How much food do we need?
4. What foods go well together?
5. What is a bargain this week?
6. What should we avoid?

*For English, see page 104; for Spanish, page 112; for French, page 126; for German, page 140.

Divide the class   Form groups of three to five students each. Give the students copies of the newspaper ads. Have the groups choose a secretary. Remind them to read over the ad for comprehension. Remind them of the questions on the blackboard.

Do the activity

Call for reports   The meals planned are reported to the class and compared.

In-class discussion topics

1. What are your favorite foods?
2. Where can we find food bargains?
3. What foods from other countries do we eat regularly?
4. Supermarkets, specialty shops, or outdoor stalls—which are the best sources of food?

Follow-up writing topics

1. Inflation and its effect on what we eat
2. Imported foods—what are they and are they important to our diet?
3. How to give a successful dinner party
4. What sort of diet is best for you?

Use this space for writing in vocabulary

Vacation—*Get me out of here!*

Objectives

To make vacation plans
To practice adverbs of time and distance
To practice travel vocabulary

Prepare   No props are necessary for this activity, but it is helpful to have on hand several road maps of different places.

Tell the class

I'm exhausted! This class has worn me out! I need a vacation, but I'm so tired that I don't have enough energy to plan for it. Since you are all expert, experienced travelers, I'm asking you to plan it for me. I don't care how much it costs.*

Check comprehension

Present vocabulary

Ask the class   What questions arise when planning a vacation? (Write the questions on the blackboard.)

1. How long is the trip?
2. Where will the teacher go? Why?
3. What methods of transportation will he or she use?
4. Will he or she stay in hotels, private homes, or camp out?
5. How will he or she pass the time?
6. What will it cost?

*For English, see page 104; for Spanish, page 112; for French, page 126; for German, page 140.

36

Divide the class   Form groups of three to five students each. Have each group choose a secretary. You may want to give each group a map and tell them to use it when planning the trip. This is a particularly useful strategy if you have maps of the country or countries being studied in the course. Remind them of the questions on the blackboard.

Do the activity

Call for reports   The secretaries announce the vacation plans. The students can vote on which is best.

In-class discussion topics

1. Why do people travel in spite of the expense?
2. Why do people take strenuous travel vacations?
3. Why do some people dislike travel?
4. How much vacation time per year does the average person need?

Follow-up writing topics

1. The best vacation I ever had
2. Planning a low-cost vacation
3. Restful versus hectic vacations
4. Practicing foreign languages while traveling abroad

Use this space for writing in vocabulary

Animal house—*Two by two*

Objectives

To practice describing animals
To practice vocabulary related to animals and their habitats

Prepare   No props are required for this activity.

Tell the class

I just received a phone call from the director of the local zoo. He told me that he is very worried because attendance at the zoo is the lowest it has ever been. It seems that the animals no longer interest the public. He asks that you, expert biologists, invent a new, more interesting animal. It would be very helpful if you could describe this animal along with its habitat, food, habits, and other special features.*

Check comprehension

Present vocabulary

Ask the class   What questions would a biologist ask about a new animal? (Write the questions on the blackboard.)

1. What does it look like?
2. In what ways does it resemble other animals?
3. What does it eat?
4. In what sort of place does it live?
5. How big is it?
6. What are its habits?
7. How do the male and female differ?

*For English, see page 104; for Spanish, page 112; for French, page 127; for German, page 141.

Divide the class   Form groups of three to five students each. Have the groups choose a secretary. Suggest that they draw the animal as well as write about it. Remind them of the questions on the blackboard.

Do the activity

Call for reports   The secretaries read the descriptions of the new animals. The sketches are shown. Encourage other students to ask questions and make comments.

In-class discussion topics

1. Why do people visit zoos?
2. Are zoos cruel to animals?
3. What are some unusual animals?
4. What limitations should be placed on scientists who try to create new types of life?

Follow-up writing topics

1. A day at the zoo
2. Building more humane zoos
3. Unusual animals
4. Taking care of rare and exotic pets

Use this space for writing in vocabulary

Student center—*I'll meet you after class*

Objectives

To consider the importance of sports and extracurricular activities to student life
To practice vocabulary relevant to student activities

Prepare   No props are required for this activity.

Tell the class

I have exciting news! The administration has selected you to design a new student center. As architects, you are to plan the most complete and up-to-date center of its kind. Spend as much money as you wish and give the students a center they will use and enjoy.*

Check comprehension

Present vocabulary

Ask the class   What questions would an architect ask about the student center? (Write the questions on the blackboard.)

1. How big will the center be?
2. What types of rooms will it have?
3. What kinds of activities will be held there?
4. What types of sports will be played there?
5. What else will people do there?
6. What special features will it have?
7. How will it be decorated?

*For English, see page 104; for Spanish, page 112; for French, page 127; for German, page 141.

Divide the class   Form groups of three to five students each. Have the groups choose a secretary. Tell them to describe the student center and, if they desire, also draw a plan. Remind them of the questions on the blackboard.

Do the activity

Call for reports   The secretaries read the descriptions and show the plans. Encourage other students to ask questions and make comments.

In-class discussion topics

1. Why are student activities important?
2. What student activities are most popular?
3. Why do students need a student center?
4. What part do sports play in education?

Follow-up writing topics

1. The ideal student center
2. The importance of extracurricular activities
3. Student clubs
4. Balancing sports, activities, and study

Use this space for writing in vocabulary

House party—*Raise the roof*

Objectives

To consider the possibilities inherent in an empty building
To practice vocabulary related to houses and public buildings

Prepare   No props are required for this activity. A large picture of a mansion would help make the activity more realistic.

Tell the class

The mayor needs your help. A wealthy bachelor has died and left his huge eighteen-room house to the city. The mayor asks that you, as architects, list the ways in which the city could use the house and then describe in detail your favorite plan.*

Check comprehension

Present vocabulary

Ask the class   What questions would an architect ask about the house? (Write the questions on the blackboard.)

1. What does the house look like?
2. Where is it located?
3. How big are the rooms?
4. What does the city need?
5. What can the house be used for?
6. What would the best use be?
7. What changes would need to be made?

*For English, see page 104; for Spanish, page 113; for French, page 127; for German, page 141.

Divide the class   Form groups of three to five students each. Have the groups choose a secretary. Remind them of the questions on the blackboard. Remind them to make a list first and then decide which use is best.

Do the activity

Call for reports   The secretaries read the lists and the plans. Encourage other students to ask questions and make comments. Summarize the results on the blackboard.

In-class discussion topics

1. How can old houses be used?
2. Where in this area are the interesting houses?
3. What social services should a city or town provide?
4. How can local officials find out what their city or town really needs?

Follow-up writing topics

1. Remodeling old houses
2. The obligations of local government
3. Improving rundown neighborhoods
4. Types of charity
5. Providing social services for the local community

Use this space for writing in vocabulary

Hobby town—*While away the hours*

Objectives

To consider enjoyable ways of spending time
To practice vocabulary related to hobbies and pastimes

Prepare   No props are required for this activity.

Tell the class

I'm bored! My old hobbies don't interest me anymore. I can't seem to think of ways to spend my free time. I'm asking you, as experts in the use of leisure time, to help me plan my free time. You should make up a list of activities that I will *really* enjoy and invent a new hobby that will definitely *not* bore me.*

Check comprehension

Present vocabulary

Ask the class   What questions would specialists in recreation need to ask? (Write the questions on the blackboard.)

1.   What hobbies can we think of?
2.   What are some very unusual hobbies?
3.   What would a new and exciting hobby be like?
4.   Could this new hobby be done alone?
5.   What materials are necessary?

*For English, see page 104; for Spanish, page 113; for French, page 127; for German, page 141.

Divide the class   Form groups of three to five students each. Have the groups choose a secretary. Remind them of the questions on the blackboard.

Do the activity

Call for reports   Have the secretaries read the lists and describe the new hobby. Summarize the results on the blackboard. Encourage other students to ask questions and make comments.

In-class discussion topics
1. Why do people have hobbies?
2. What hobbies do you have?
3. Why do some people spend large amounts of money on their hobbies?
4. Which hobbies are most popular? Why?

Follow-up writing topics
1. My hobbies
2. Entertaining yourself
3. Unusual hobbies and pastimes
4. Expensive and inexpensive hobbies

Use this space for writing in vocabulary

Chef—*It's delicious!*

Objectives

To think about food in a fanciful manner
To practice food and cooking vocabulary

Prepare   No props are required for this activity. However, a few photographs of gourmet meals could help set the mood. The meals pictured should be very extravagant. Photographs of this sort can be found in magazines directed to gourmet cooks.

Tell the class

Congratulations! The Chefs' Academy has chosen you, all master chefs, to plan the menu for the graduation banquet. Your choice of ingredients is limitless. You may plan anything, but whatever you serve must be interesting to look at and very extravagant. Do not be afraid to invent new dishes.*

Check comprehension

Present vocabulary

Ask the class   What questions do chefs ask? (Write the questions on the blackboard.)

1. How many courses will we have?
2. What will we have for the appetizer? soup? salad? main dish? dessert?
3. What will we serve to drink?
4. What special ingredients will we need?

*For English, see page 104; for Spanish, page 113; for French, page 128; for German, page 142.

Divide the class   Form groups of three to five students each. Have each group choose a secretary. Tell them that if they wish, they may draw pictures. Remind them of the questions on the blackboard.

Do the activity

Call for reports   The secretaries describe the dishes and show the pictures. Encourage other students to ask questions and make comments. Summarize the results.

In-class discussion topics

1. What do you like to cook?
2. Why has gourmet cooking become popular?
3. Why, besides to eat, do people go to restaurants?
4. What type of person makes a good chef?

Follow-up writing topics

1. Being a chef
2. Gourmet cooking as a hobby
3. A dish I invented
4. Working in a restaurant

Use this space for writing in vocabulary

Floating—*I love a parade*

Objectives

To design a three-dimensional creation
To practice vocabulary dealing with shapes, sizes, and colors

Prepare   No props are required for this activity

Tell the class

I am pleased to announce that this class has been chosen to design a float for the Founder's Day parade. The Parade Committee says that you can plan to spend as much as you wish and that you may use any materials that you like. The floats will be judged for creativity and beauty by a group of celebrities. You will need to describe your float and also create a working sketch.*

Check comprehension

Present vocabulary

Ask the class   What questions do you need to ask about the float? (Write the questions on the blackboard.)

1. How big is it?
2. What colors will we use?
3. What materials will we use?
4. How many people will ride on it?
5. What will it look like?
6. What symbols will be on it?
7. How will we move it?

*For English, see page 104; for Spanish, page 114; for French, page 128; for German, page 142.

Divide the class   Form groups of three to five students each. Have the groups choose a secretary. Remind them of the questions on the blackboard.

Do the activity

Call for reports   The secretaries read the descriptions and show the sketches. Encourage other students to ask questions and make comments.

In-class discussion topics

1. Why do people build floats?
2. Why are local celebrations important?
3. Why are parades popular?
4. When are parades held here?

Follow-up writing topics

1. Building a float
2. Organizing a parade
3. Local holidays
4. Developing community spirit

Use this space for writing in vocabulary

Toyland—*Let's play!*

Objectives

To consider the difficulties of entertaining children
To practice vocabulary related to toys and games

Prepare   No props are required for this activity.

Tell the class

My friend Richard needs your advice! His young nieces and nephews are coming to stay with him. Richard is a bachelor with no children. He owns no toys at all. He would like to get some toys for the children to play with, but he can't afford to spend much and has no idea of what children like. He asks you, educational consultants, to suggest a list of toys and games that will be fun, safe, and inexpensive. At least one of these toys and games should be your own invention.*

Check comprehension

Present vocabulary

Ask the class   What questions do we need to ask about toys and games? (Write the questions on the blackboard.)

1. Which toys are safe, fun, and inexpensive?
2. What are they made of?
3. What colors are they?
4. Are they powered? How?
5. How can we make a new toy of cheap or used materials?
6. What would a new game be like?

*For English, see page 105; for Spanish, page 114; for French, page 128; for German, page 142.

Divide the class   Form groups of three to five students each. Have the groups choose a secretary. Remind them of the questions on the blackboard.

Do the activity   Remind them to make a list of toys and games and then invent a new one.

Call for reports   The secretaries read the lists of toys and games and the descriptions of what their groups have invented. Summarize the results. Encourage other students to ask questions and make comments.

In-class discussion topics

1. Which toys do you remember best?
2. What kind of toys are most popular with younger children? With older children?
3. Why are toys important?
4. Which games are most popular with younger children? With older children?
5. Should children be allowed to play with guns and other "war toys"?

Follow-up writing topics

1. Making children's toys
2. Popular children's toys and games
3. Buying the appropriate toys for children
4. Improving kindergartens and day care centers

Use this space for writing in vocabulary

Snake oil—*It cures all*

Objectives

To consider medicine, illness, and doctors
To practice medical vocabulary

Prepare   No props are required for this activity.

Tell the class

It's hard to be a doctor these days! It's very frustrating! After so many years
of medical discoveries, there are still too many diseases that the doctors
can't cure. A new "wonder drug" is what they need. It's up to you, as expert
chemists, to develop a new medicine which will cure a multitude of diseases
and medical conditions.*

Check comprehension

Present vocabulary   Review vocabulary relating to being sick such as: to
have a headache, to get sick.

Ask the class   What questions would a chemist ask? (Write the questions
on the blackboard.)

1. What diseases will the medicine cure?
2. For what other conditions will the medicine be effective?
3. What dosage do we recommend?
4. What will it be called?
5. Where can it be obtained?

*For English, see page 105; for Spanish, page 114; for French, page 128; for German, page 143.

Divide the class   Form groups of three to five students each. Tell them that they are working for important laboratories. Have each group choose a secretary. Remind them of the questions on the blackboard.

Do the activity

Call for reports   The secretaries acting as the leaders of the laboratory teams read their reports about the new "wonder drugs." Encourage other students to ask questions and make comments. Summarize the results.

In-class discussion topics

1. Which diseases are still incurable?
2. For which diseases have cures been recently found?
3. Are drug companies too powerful?
4. Why do doctors have so much prestige?

Follow-up writing topics

1. Recent medical developments
2. Ancient methods of medical treatment
3. Being a health professional (doctor, nurse, chiropractor, physical therapist)
4. The time I was seriously ill

Use this space for writing in vocabulary

Planning board—*I propose . . .*

Objectives

To give students a chance to do urban planning
To practice vocabulary relating to civic affairs

Prepare   No props are required for this activity.

Tell the class

The situation in Horaceton is a disgrace! Years of mismanagement by the mayor and city council have led to urban blight and decay. Fortunately, a new reform administration has just taken over and all of you are to serve on the new planning board. Several important projects need to be done right away. Among them are a city-wide clean-up, a noise reduction program, and the building of a new rapid transit system. The plans should be innovative and original. Let's make Horaceton a model city!*

Variation   Where appropriate, add local problems to the list.

Check comprehension

Present vocabulary

Reinforce grammar   Practice comparatives.

Ask the class   What questions do city planners have to answer? (Write the questions on the blackboard.)

1. What needs to be done?
2. What changes are necessary?
3. What has to be done first?
4. What is the most interesting way to do it?
5. What is the easiest way to do it?

*For English, see page 105; for Spanish, page 114; for French, page 129; for German, page 143.

Divide the class   Form groups of three to five students each. Assign one of the projects to each group. Have each group choose a secretary. Remind them of the questions on the blackboard.

Do the activity

Call for reports   The secretaries read the plans. Encourage other students to ask questions and make comments.

In-class discussion topics
1. How can city life be improved?
2. Why do cities decay?
3. What should city planners remember?
4. How can citizens get involved in city or town planning?

Follow-up writing topics
1. City planning—does it really work?
2. The city of the future
3. Improving rapid transit
4. Getting involved in local politics

Use this space for writing in vocabulary

Shipwreck—*A tropical paradise*

Objectives

To consider issues of survival
To practice dealing with a crisis situation

Prepare   No props are required for this activity. However, to make the activity more realistic, bring to class pocket knives, matches, wire, and a small first aid kit.

Tell the class

I was right! I wanted to fly to Tahiti, but you all insisted on going by ship. The ship sank during a terrible Pacific storm. We're all lucky to be alive! Somehow, we were able to reach a deserted island. The climate here is pleasant and there is much vegetation. There are no other people on the island. All we have are the clothing we are wearing, matches, knives, wire, and a few medicines. We've got to organize ourselves. We need a plan. It could be a long time before help arrives.*

Check comprehension

Present vocabulary

Ask the class   What questions would a group of shipwrecked people have to ask before they could get organized? (Write the questions on the blackboard.)

1. Where are we?
2. What is available here?
3. What do we have?
4. What skills do we have?
5. How can we feed, clothe, and shelter ourselves?
6. How should we organize ourselves?
7. How can we call for help?

*For English, see page 105; for Spanish, page 115; for French, page 129; for German, page 143.

Divide the class   Form groups of three to five students each. Have each group choose a secretary. Remind them of the questions on the blackboard. Tell them to make a survival plan.

Do the activity

Call for reports   The secretaries read their survival plans. Encourage other students to ask questions and make comments. Summarize the results.

In-class discussion topics

1.   What do we really need in order to survive? What are the basic necessities?
2.   Why do some people survive a crisis while others don't?
3.   Could you survive on a desert island?
4.   Was your life ever endangered? How did you get through the situation?
5.   What type of political organization works best during crisis situations?

Follow-up writing topics

1.   Getting back to basics—what we have that we could live without
2.   Dealing with emergency
3.   My scariest moment
4.   Preparing for the unexpected

Use this space for writing in vocabulary

Zodiac—*It's in the stars*

Objectives

To look at astrology in a new way
To practice using descriptive adjectives which apply to people
To practice use of the future tense

Prepare   This activity can be done without props. However, it will be more effective if you bring to class a sample horoscope written in the target language. These can often be found in newspapers or popular magazines. You could translate a sample horoscope from one of the numerous books that are available on the subject. If possible, make copies of the sample horoscope for all of the students.

Tell the class

It has happened again! A horoscope was completely wrong! Not only that, more and more people claim that their personalities do not fit those associated with the traditional signs of the zodiac such as Aries, the ram, and Leo, the lion. Since you are all expert astrologers, you can help. You have the knowledge necessary so that you can identify new signs of the zodiac and describe the personality characteristics of those people who were born under them.*

Check comprehension

Present vocabulary   Review the names of animals and birds.

Ask the class   What questions do astrologers ask? (Write the questions on the blackboard.)

1. What is the name of the sign? What are its dates?
2. What are the characteristics of the animal or bird?
3. What type of person has these qualities?
4. How does this person act and feel?
5. How do other people view this person?
6. What is this person's future going to be like?

*For English, see page 105; for Spanish, page 115; for French, page 129; for German, page 143.

Divide the class   Form groups of three to five students each. Have the groups choose a secretary. Tell them to describe one new sign. Remind them of the questions on the blackboard.

Do the activity

Call for reports   The secretaries read about the new signs of the zodiac. Encourage other students to ask questions and make comments. Ask if any of the new signs correctly describe people in the class.

In-class discussion topics

1. Is astrology nonsense?
2. Why do people believe in astrology?
3. Have you ever had your chart read?
4. What other methods do people use to predict the future?

Follow-up writing topics

1. Explaining the popularity of astrology
2. Predicting the future
3. Consulting an astrologer
4. Personality types

Use this space for writing in vocabulary

Tribal council—*We must deliberate*

Objectives

To give students an opportunity to do social planning
To practice vocabulary relating to government and society

Prepare   No props are required for this activity.

Tell the class

I have terrible news! As a result of a decree from the government, you must leave the lands your people have lived in for generations and move to another area. Since you are the elders of the tribe, you must plan for a profound change in the tribe's way of life. There will be limited resources there. If things are properly managed, the tribe will prosper. If not, disaster will result. The plans you make now will affect future generations.*

Check comprehension

Present vocabulary

Ask the class   What questions should the council try to answer? (Write the questions on the blackboard.)

1. What will the new site be like?—land, climate, size?
2. What kind of government will be necessary?
3. How will we organize the people?
4. What industries or agriculture should be emphasized?

*For English, see page 105; for Spanish, page 115; for French, page 130; for German, page 144.

Divide the class Form groups of three to five students each. Have each group choose a secretary. Each student should have a chance to propose a solution and answer each question *as an elder.* (They could even choose new names.) They should agree by vote or consensus. Remind them of the questions on the blackboard.

Do the activity

Call for reports The secretaries report the tribal council's decision. The results are compared. Encourage other students to ask questions and make comments.

In-class discussion topics
1. Social planning—can it work?
2. Should reservations be abolished?
3. How do people react to disasters?

Follow-up writing topics
1. The uses of social planning
2. Reacting to crisis
3. The difficulties of moving to a place quite different from your home

---

Use this space for writing in vocabulary

Sell–Sell–Sell—*Get rid of it!*

Quick sale—*I need the money*

Objectives

To practice writing advertising
To practice imperatives and superlatives

Prepare   No props are required for this activity.

Tell the class

I have urgent news! Tuition (or school fees) has been increased. To avoid collection problems, the administration has declared that students must pay the difference immediately. In order to raise the money, you must sell to your classmates something that you have with you now. You'll have to write advertising that will make them want to buy what you're selling.*

Check comprehension

Present vocabulary

Reinforce grammar   If students know the imperative forms, review them here. If not, review forms like "you should buy." Review superlatives.

Ask the class   What will you need to say? (Write the questions on the blackboard.)

1.   What am I selling?
2.   Why should you want to buy it?
3.   What is the quality?
4.   How can you contact me?
5.   What is the price?

*For English, see page 105; for Spanish, page 116; for French, page 130; for German, page 144.

Do the activity   The students write for five minutes.

Call for reports   Each student reads a sales pitch to the class. They may set prices or ask for offers. They can answer questions from other students. An auction may be held.

In-class discussion topics

1. How can we earn money for school?
2. Tuition rates—are they fair?
3. Should education be free?
4. How can we get money in an emergency?

Follow-up writing topics

1. How to pay for a college education
2. Working and going to school—do they mix?
3. Money-raising techniques

Use this space for writing in vocabulary

Soft soap—*Stronger than dirt*

Objectives

To practice being persuasive
To practice imperatives
To practice vocabulary dealing with cleanliness

Prepare This activity can be done without props, but it will be more interesting if samples of cleansers, polishes, stain removers, and laundry detergents in unmarked wrappers are brought to class.

Tell the class

We're in luck! Our advertising agency, Fee, Fie, Foe and Fum, has just been hired by the XYZ Detergent Company. This company insists that its products are better and stronger than anything now on the market. They have extraordinary powers. It's your job as the best advertising writers around to write ads that will attract many new customers to XYZ products.*

Check comprehension

Present vocabulary

Reinforce grammar   Review imperatives.

Ask the class   What questions will the ads have to answer? (Write the questions on the blackboard.)

1. What is being sold?
2. Why is it better? Unusual?
3. What can it do?
4. Why buy now?
5. How much does it cost?
6. Where is it sold?

*For English, see page 105; for Spanish, page 116; for French, page 130; for German, page 144.

Divide the class   Form groups of three to five students each. Have each group choose a secretary. Each group can write about a different product (soap, polish, detergent) or the groups can compete in writing about a single product. If you have samples, you can pass them around. You may want to specify a certain kind of advertising, such as radio, TV, or magazine. You could suggest that the ads be sung or read aloud in chorus. Remind them of the questions on the blackboard.

Do the activity

Call for reports   The secretaries or the entire group read the ads. The class can vote on which ad is best.

In-class discussion topics

1. Is advertising really helpful to the public?
2. Should all advertising be completely honest?
3. How many choices of products are really needed?
4. What type of advertising is most effective?

Follow-up writing topics

1. Planning an advertising campaign
2. Truth in advertising—is it possible?
3. An effective ad
4. A world without advertising

Use this space for writing in vocabulary

Used car—*Unload it!*

Objectives

To practice talking about automobiles
To mimic the style of automobile advertising
To practice automobile vocabulary

Prepare   No props are required for this activity.

Tell the class

I've got a problem! I've been trying to sell my car for six months now, but no one wants to buy it. It runs well and I'm asking a fair price, but people keep telling me that it is too weird, too strange, and too different. You are my last hope! I'm asking you, as specialists in writing advertising, to compose an ad that will be guaranteed to sell my car.

Oh! I forgot to bring my picture of the car, but I'm sure you can imagine what my very unusual car is like. You may even want to draw a picture of it.*

Check comprehension

Present vocabulary

Reinforce grammar   Practice superlatives; review imperatives.

Ask the class   What does an automobile ad usually include? (Write the questions on the blackboard.)

1. What kind of car is it?
2. What is its make, model, and year?
3. What special features does it have?
4. How many miles has it been driven?
5. What condition is it in?
6. What is the price?
7. How can the owner be contacted?

*For English, see page 105; for Spanish, page 116; for French, page 131; for German, page 145.

Divide the class   Form groups of three to five students each. Have each group choose a secretary. Remind them of the questions on the blackboard.

Do the activity

Call for reports   The secretaries read the ads to the class. Encourage other students to ask questions and make comments. Summarize the results.

In-class discussion topics
1. Why buy a used car?
2. Is it safe to buy a used car?
3. What should you look for in a used car?
4. What happens if something goes wrong with a used car after it has been sold?

Follow-up writing topics
1. The advantages of buying a used car
2. The dangers of buying a used car
3. How to avoid being cheated when buying a used car
4. Selling your car

Use this space for writing in vocabulary

Alma mater—*Hail to thee!*

Objectives

To give students an opportunity to evaluate their school or program
To practice education-related vocabulary

Prepare   No props are required for this activity.

Tell the class

Our beloved school is in serious trouble! So few new students will be coming here next year that many programs will have to be cancelled. If the problem continues for a few years, the entire school will have to be closed. Only you can help. Since you love the school and know all of its good points, you are the ideal people to write the advertising that will attract new students and convince students who have left to return.*

Check comprehension

Present vocabulary

Ask the class   What questions should your ad answer? (Write the questions on the blackboard.)

1. Where is the school located?
2. What is special about it?
3. What special programs are offered?
4. What sports facilities are available?
5. What extracurricular programs are available?
6. How will this school help the students' employment possibilities?

*For English, see page 105; for Spanish, page 117; for French, page 131; for German, page 145.

Divide the class   Form groups of three to five students each. Have each group choose a secretary. Remind them of the questions on the blackboard.

Do the activity

Call for reports   The secretaries read the ads. Encourage other students to ask questions and make comments.

In-class discussion topics

1. Should schools and colleges recruit students?
2. How do students choose a school or college?
3. How do schools differ?
4. Why are people loyal to their schools?

Follow-up writing topics

1. The effects of declining enrollments
2. Recruiting students
3. Changing schools to meet student needs
4. Choosing the right school

Use this space for writing in vocabulary

Campaign—*The people's choice!*

Objectives

To practice talking about politics
To practice using vocabulary, especially adjectives, related to politics
To use superlatives and exaggerated speech

Prepare   No props are necessary for this activity.

Tell the class

In my opinion, none of the candidates for the next election is any good. There are no great candidates any more. In response to this, I've arranged for you to nominate anyone you like from the present day or from the past to run for this important office. The people you choose don't have to be politicians, they don't have to be from this country, and they don't have to be alive or even to have existed at all. They may be very unusual. You need to pick a candidate and then make up campaign slogans and political literature which support the candidate.*

Check comprehension

Present vocabulary

Reinforce grammar   Review superlatives. Discuss the ways in which exaggerating can be done.

Ask the class   What questions will you have to ask before writing campaign materials? (Write the questions on the blackboard.)

1. Who is our candidate?
2. What does this candidate support?
3. Why should someone vote for this candidate?
4. What has this candidate done in the past?
5. What plans does this candidate have?
6. When are the elections?
7. Where should people go in order to vote?

*For English, see page 106; for Spanish, page 117; for French, page 131; for German, page 145.

Divide the class   There are two ways to begin this activity.

1. The whole class suggests five candidates whose names are written on the blackboard. Ask the students to choose the candidate they would like to support. Form groups of three to five students each, balancing the groups as necessary. Have each group choose a secretary. Remind them of the questions on the blackboard.

2. Form groups of three to five students each. Have each group choose a secretary. Tell the groups to agree on a candidate and then write campaign materials in support of their choice. Remind them of the questions on the blackboard.

Do the activity

Call for reports   The secretaries read the campaign slogans and materials their groups have made up. Encourage other students to react to the messages.

In-class discussion topics

1. Are good candidates running for public office? Who?
2. Should there be laws restricting political advertising? Why? How?
3. Are people persuaded by campaign slogans? In what ways?
4. What restrictions, if any, should be placed on candidates for public office?
5. Should anyone who wants to run for office be allowed to do so?

Follow-up writing topics

1. Writing political publicity
2. Taking part in a political campaign
3. Election laws
4. The strengths and weaknesses of the electoral system

Use this space for writing in vocabulary

Tourist office—*See the sights*

Objectives

To practice describing places
To use persuasive language
To practice vocabulary relating to vacations and tourism

Prepare   No props are required for this activity.

Tell the class

I am delighted to welcome you, representatives of the Tourism Ministries of your countries, to the United Nations conference in honor of the "Year of the Tourist." As you all know, rising travel costs threaten the future of the tourist industries and therefore the economies of your countries. Your task, while attending this conference, is to formulate new and persuasive descriptions of the virtues of your countries which will attract prospective tourists.

The representatives of Richlandia, Midlandia, and Poorlandia will meet separately to prepare their materials. Later, we will meet again and test them on the rest of the group.*

Check comprehension

Present vocabulary

Ask the class   What questions will tourism officials need to answer? (Write the questions on the blackboard.)

1. What are the advantages to the tourist in our country?
2. Which tourists should we attract?
3. How expensive is travel in our country?
4. Are there inexpensive ways to travel in our country?
5. Do we offer special deals?
6. How can a tourist get to our country?
7. When is the best time of year to travel to our country?

---

*For English, see page 106; for Spanish, page 117; for French, page 131; for German, page 146.

Divide the class Divide the class into groups of three to five students each. Designate each group as the representatives of one of the three countries (Richlandia, Midlandia, Poorlandia). If practical, you can allow the students to choose the country they want to work on. Try to have an equal number of groups working on each country. Have each group choose a secretary. Remind them of the questions on the blackboard.

Do the activity

Call for reports The secretaries or the groups as a whole read the advertisements. Encourage other students to ask questions and make comments.

In-class discussion topics

1. Why do people take trips?
2. How do countries benefit from tourism?
3. What would make an ideal tourist resort?
4. Where is your favorite place?

Follow-up writing topics

1. My most memorable trip
2. Promoting tourism
3. The disadvantages of tourism to the host country
4. Traveling cheaply

Use this space for writing in vocabulary

Mansion—*A house is not a home*

Objectives

To describe houses and other forms of real estate
To use persuasive language
To practice vocabulary related to buildings and real estate transactions
To practice speaking about shapes, sizes, and measurements

Prepare　　Select several photographs or drawings of obviously very expensive dwellings such as castles and mansions. Pictures of such places can regularly be found in the real estate section of major daily newspapers and in magazines catering to people with expensive tastes.

Tell the class

I just can't understand it! These *beautiful* houses have been on the market for months now, but no one wants to buy them. The real estate brokers are very frustrated. They are asking you, experts in selling real estate, to write advertising that will attract buyers. If the houses are sold, you'll get a big commission.*

Check comprehension

Present vocabulary　　Practice using measurements.

Reinforce grammar　　Review comparatives.

Ask the class　　What questions will you answer in your ads? (Write the questions on the blackboard.)

1. What is the house like?
2. What special features does it have?
3. Why is it a good buy?
4. Where is it located?
5. What price is being asked?
6. Who is the real estate broker?
7. How can the real estate broker be contacted?

*For English, see page 106; for Spanish, page 118; for French, page 132; for German, page 146.

Divide the class   Form groups of three to five students each. Tell each group to choose the house they want to advertise. Have each group choose a secretary. Remind them of the questions on the blackboard.

Do the activity   The groups write their ads. If time permits, they could also write a dialogue between a real estate broker and a potential buyer.

Call for reports   The secretaries read the ads. Encourage other students to ask questions and make comments about the ads.

In-class discussion topics

1. Why do people buy mansions?
2. What do real estate agents do?
3. Where are there bargains on real estate?
4. What does your ideal home look like?

Follow-up writing topics

1. Buying and selling real estate
2. My perfect home
3. Unusual homes
4. Living in an apartment versus living in a house

Use this space for writing in vocabulary

Air waves—Listen in!

Objectives

To make fun of radio advertising
To consider the role radio plays in daily life
To use persuasive language

Prepare   No props are required for this activity.

Tell the class

The owners of radio station WXXX are very worried. Fewer people are listening to the station than ever before. Unless the station gets more listeners soon, it will have to close. Only you, expert consultants, can save the station. Your job is to write radio advertising which will attract new listeners. You may also make up games and contests that can be played on the air and suggest new programs. Let's save WXXX!*

Check comprehension

Present vocabulary

Ask the class   What questions will advertising writers need to answer? (Write the questions on the blackboard.)

1. Why should someone listen to WXXX?
2. What is different about WXXX?
3. How can we make the ads funny?
4. What type of game would listeners want to play?
5. Where is WXXX on the dial?

---

*For English, see page 106; for Spanish, page 118; for French, page 132; for German, page 146.

Divide the class   Form groups of three to five students each. Have each group choose a secretary. Tell them to write the ad before they make up a contest. Remind them of the questions on the blackboard.

Do the activity

Call for reports   The secretaries read or sing the ads. They report on any contests or program changes that their group has planned. Encourage other students to ask questions and make comments.

In-class discussion topics
1. Why is radio so popular?
2. What is your favorite type of radio program?
3. Why do advertisers use radio?
4. How should radio stations go about attracting more listeners?

Follow-up writing topics
1. Improving advertising on the radio
2. Government control of the air
3. The importance of local radio
4. Listener-sponsored (public) radio

Use this space for writing in vocabulary

Last rites—*Bury the dead*

Objectives

To practice describing people and their accomplishments
To become acquainted with the format of obituaries
To practice vocabulary related to funerals

Prepare   Select examples of obituaries written in the target language. Choose obituaries of people who had been famous or at least a bit unusual. This sort of obituary is commonly found in the international editions of newspapers. If these are not available, make up a sample obituary for a real or fictional person. Make a copy of the obituary for each student.

Tell the class

I have very sad news! Several internationally known figures have all suddenly died. Among them are: the Honorable Alphonsus Muggeridge, ex-ambassador from the Republic of Wellingtonia to the United States; Max "The Fly" Jones, infamous murderer, jewel thief, and member of the Uptown Gang; and Dame Edith Harshtone, soloist for the Western Opera Company. However, these deaths shall not pass unnoticed. As skilled journalists, you have been given the honor of writing the obituaries for these important people.*

Check comprehension

Present vocabulary

Give an example   Hand out copies of the obituaries. Read them aloud and go over the significant features.

*For English, see page 106; for Spanish, page 118; for French, page 132; for German, page 147.

Ask the class   What questions will you have to ask before writing an obituary? (Write the questions on the blackboard.)

1. Who died?
2. When?
3. How old was he or she?
4. What were his or her accomplishments?
5. Is the death greatly mourned?
6. Where will the funeral be held? When?
7. Who may attend the funeral?
8. What will the funeral be like?
9. Who are the survivors?

Divide the class   Form groups of three to five students each. If convenient, allow the students to choose the person about whom they want to write. Otherwise, divide the class arbitrarily. Have the groups choose a secretary. Remind them of the questions on the blackboard.

Do the activity

Call for reports   The secretaries read the obituaries. Encourage other students to ask questions and make comments.

In-class discussion topics

1. Why are obituaries written? Wouldn't a simple announcement of death be sufficient?
2. How do obituaries differ?
3. What are some of the ways in which respect is paid for the dead?
4. How do funerals differ?
5. Should funerals of public figures be open to the public or limited to the family of the deceased?

Follow-up writing topics

1. Showing respect for the dead
2. Styles of obituaries
3. Types of funerals
4. The importance of memorial ceremonies

Use this space for writing in vocabulary

Dead language—*How do you say?*

Objectives

To consider the reasons for foreign language study
To consider the reasons that students do not take foreign language courses
To practice using persuasive language
To practice writing to authorities

Prepare   No props are required for this activity.

Tell the class

I've just received some disturbing news. Enrollments in classes of Hondari, the language of Hondaristan, have been dropping drastically. Students are no longer signing up to study this formerly popular language. School officials are threatening to cancel the entire Hondari program. The chairman of the Foreign Languages Department has urgently requested that you, so dedicated to foreign language study, and experts in many languages, write a letter to the administration in which you explain why Hondari should be taught and suggest ways of attracting students to Hondari classes.*

Check comprehension

Present vocabulary

Ask the class   What questions will you have to ask before you write your letter supporting the teaching of Hondari? (Write the questions on the blackboard.)

1. Where is Hondaristan?
2. Why is it important?
3. What does it produce?
4. What is Hondaristani culture like?
5. What are the advantages of knowing Hondari?
6. How will the students be affected if Hondari is not taught?
7. What would attract students to Hondari classes?

*For English, see page 106; for Spanish, page 119; for French, page 133; for German, page 147.

Divide the class   Form groups of three to five students each. Have each group choose a secretary. Remind them of the questions on the blackboard.

Do the activity

Call for reports   The secretaries read the letters to the class. Encourage other students to ask questions and make comments. Summarize the arguments on the blackboard.

In-class discussion topics
1. Why should people study foreign languages?
2. Should foreign language study be required?
3. What is the best age to study a foreign language?
4. How can people be encouraged to learn languages that are not commonly studied?
5. How can knowledge of a foreign language be useful on the job?

Follow-up writing topics
1. The language requirement
2. The importance of foreign language study
3. Recruiting students for foreign language courses
4. Improving foreign language education

Use this space for writing in vocabulary

Impersonate—*Act it out!*

Taxi driver—*Where are you from?*

Objectives

To simulate the experience of being in a foreign country
To practice making someone's acquaintance

Prepare   No props are required for this activity.

Tell the class

After an exhausting seven-hour flight, you have finally arrived in the city of Wallen, the capital of Contursia. With some luck, you find a taxi. You are a little nervous because you don't know a word of Contursi and the driver doesn't know any of your native language. However, you quickly learn that the driver has been studying the same language that you have and coincidently knows exactly as much of it as you do. It's a long ride from the airport to the center of the city so you will have ample time to get to know each other.*

Variation   With only slight modification, this activity could be done around a barber, a beautician, a bellhop, or a waiter.

Check comprehension

Present vocabulary

Ask the class   What questions would the tourist and the driver ask each other? (Write the questions on the blackboard.)

Driver
1. Where are you coming from?
2. Where do you live?
3. Is this your first visit to Contursia?
4. Do you have any relatives in Contursia?
5. Do you know my cousin who lives in your country?

*For English, see page 106; for Spanish, page 119; for French, page 133; for German, page 147.

Tourist

1. What should I see?
2. What should I buy? Where can I get bargains?
3. Where should I eat?
4. How has the weather been?
5. Have you lived here all your life?
6. What do you think of the political situation in Contursia?

Divide the class   Have the students pair off. It can be helpful to match a weak student with a strong one, but it is not necessary. Tell them that one of them is to be the tourist and the other is to be the taxi driver.

Do the activity   In elementary classes, students should write down the dialogue as they create it. In more advanced classes, students can act out the parts and then write down some of their conversation.

Call for reports   Students read the dialogues to the class. They should be urged to act as much as they can. Advanced students can expand upon their written dialogues.

In-class discussion topics

1. Have you been in a situation like the one in this activity?
2. How much foreign language does a traveler need to know?
3. How can you make yourself understood when you don't know the language?
4. What topics should you avoid speaking about when you are in another country?

Follow-up writing topics

1. The difficulties of foreign travel
2. Culture shock
3. Getting around in another country

Use this space for writing in vocabulary

Tour guide—*I know a place*

Objectives

To become more aware of local landmarks and attractions
To practice giving directions
To practice describing places

Prepare   This activity can be done without props. Having a few local tourist maps on hand would make it more realistic.

Tell the class

I have a favor to ask of you. My uncle is coming to spend some time visiting the area. It's his first trip here and he wants to see all the sights. Unfortunately, I'll have very little free time next week. Besides, I don't know the area very well. Since you are all experienced tour guides, you can explain the local sights to my uncle. I'd really appreciate it.*

Variations
1. The visitor could be someone other than the teacher's uncle.
2. The city described could be the students' home town.
3. The city described could be imaginary.

Check comprehension

Present vocabulary

Ask the class   What questions would the tour guide and the visitor ask each other? (Write the questions on the blackboard.)

Tour guide
1. What have you heard about this area?
2. What are you most interested in seeing?
3. How much time do you have?

Visitor
1. What is this area famous for?
2. What should I see first?
3. Where should I spend most of my time?

*For English, see page 106; for Spanish, page 119; for French, page 133; for German, page 148.

Divide the class   This activity can be organized in three different ways.

1. Have the students pair off. It can be helpful to match a stronger student with a weaker one, but this is not necessary. Tell the students to choose parts with one student as the tour guide and the other as the visitor. Have them practice acting out the parts and then write out the dialogue they have created. Remind them of the questions on the blackboard.

2. Form groups of three to five students each. Have the groups choose a secretary. Have the groups write out a dialogue between a tour guide and a visitor. Remind them of the questions on the blackboard.

3. Form groups of three to five students each. Have the groups choose a secretary. Tell them that they should plan a tour of the area for the visitor. Help them rephrase the questions on the board to meet their needs as tour planners.

Do the activity

Call for reports   The pairs or groups read and act out the dialogues they have written. Or, the secretaries read the plans for the visitor. Encourage other students to ask questions and make comments.

In-class discussion topics

1. Why should anyone visit this area?
2. Is it possible to be a tourist in your own home town?
3. When you're visiting a new place, is it better to have a guide or see the sights by yourself? Why?
4. What problems do tour guides face?

Follow-up writing topics

1. The tourist attractions in my home town
2. Planning a visit to another city
3. Writing a tourist guidebook
4. The art of being a tour guide

Use this space for writing in vocabulary

Visiting scholar—*In my country . . .*

Objectives

To simulate being a student in another country
To practice asking basic questions

Prepare   No props are required for this activity.

Tell the class

I have wonderful news! You have all won scholarships to spend a year in a
country where the language being taught in this course is spoken. The only
requirement is that during the time there, you speak only the language we've
been studying. Since this will be difficult, it would be a good idea for you to
form self-help groups and begin meeting and practicing before you leave. In
these groups, you can discuss how to deal with problems such as finding
housing, getting around the country, trying the food, meeting local people,
and enrolling in a school or university. There is no time to lose. You should
get started right away.*

Variations

1. Students resident in a country where the target language is spoken can, in
effect, play themselves. They can discuss experiences they have had and
exchange information.

2. Students can act the part of visiting foreign students who have just arrived.
Since they come from different countries, speak different languages, and don't yet
know the language of the country they are visiting, they must converse in the
language being taught in this course. Back home, they had all studied exactly the
same amount of it.

Check comprehension

Present vocabulary

*For English, see page 106; for Spanish, page 120; for French, page 134; for German, page 148.

Ask the class   What questions do foreign students need to ask? (Write the questions on the blackboard.)

1. How can I find a place to live?
2. How can I travel around the city?
3. What do I need to do in order to enroll in a school or university?
4. What do I do in an emergency?
5. Where can I get good food?
6. Where are the bank, the train station, and the police station?
7. Where can I buy inexpensive clothing?

Divide the class   Form groups of three to five students each. Have each group choose a secretary. Tell them to identify the country they will be visiting. Remind them of the questions on the blackboard.

Do the activity

Call for reports   Ask the secretaries to tell about their group's discussion. Summarize the discussions.

In-class discussion topics

1. Why do people study in other countries?
2. What types of students study in other countries?
3. What are the most difficult problems faced by foreign students?
4. When learning a language, is it necessary to go to a country where that language is spoken? Why or why not?

Follow-up writing topics

1. The problems faced by a foreign student
2. Making a little bit of a foreign language go a long way
3. Organized programs and other ways of studying abroad
4. Tips for the foreign student

Use this space for writing in vocabulary

Nostalgia—*Remember the days*

Objectives

To practice greetings
To practice chatting and small talk
To consider changes that could take place during twenty-five years
To practice the past tenses and ways of talking of time past

Prepare   This activity can be done well without props, but an old high school yearbook and banner would help set the mood.

Tell the class

You all have been fortunate enough to have been invited to the twenty-fifth reunion of the Jasmine High School Class of 19 _____ . Since you were all members of that class, I'm sure you will be delighted to see your old friends and chat about the changes you've undergone in the past twenty-five years. Try to remember gossip from those good old days at Jasmine High.*

Variations

1. (*continue*) Since I'm the only one who knows you both then and now, I'll remind you of who you have been. (Choose students to be the prom queen, football hero, class president, once-shy person now a movie star, the "bad kid" now chief of police, the aging English teacher who remembers them all, the star of the senior play, the retired coach, the cheerleaders, the average kids.)

If the class is small give each student a different identity. In larger classes, it's possible to repeat identities.

2. The students are invited to the reunion of *this* class as it might take place twenty-five years from now. They attend as older versions of themselves.

Check comprehension

Present vocabulary

Reinforce grammar   Include past tenses, contrasts between tenses, ways of saying "ago."

---

*For English, see page 106; for Spanish, page 120; for French, page 134; for German, page 148.

Ask the class   What questions are you likely to ask someone you haven't seen for twenty-five years? (Write the questions on the blackboard.)

1. How are you?
2. How have you been?
3. Where have you been?
4. Do you remember how we used to _____ ?
5. Whatever happened to _____ ?
6. How long ago did you _____ ?
7. How long have you _____ ?

Divide the class   With a smaller class it may be possible to do this as a whole-class activity. Or, divide the class into groups of about eight. If space permits, allow the class to stand and walk around the room so as to be as realistic as possible. Remind them of the questions on the blackboard.

Do the activity   You may join as a member of the class or as a former teacher. At the end of about fifteen minutes, ask some students what they've learned about the others.

In-class discussion topics

1. What are reunions for?
2. Why do people attend reunions after many years?
3. What about a person changes the most?
4. What changes the least?
5. Why do some friendships pass the test of time?

Follow-up writing topics

1. Why people should (not) attend reunions
2. The importance of the high school years
3. The friends I remember
4. What nostalgia really is

Use this space for writing in vocabulary

High society—*You are cordially invited*

Objectives

To practice formal greetings, leave-taking, and introductions
To practice small talk and gossip

Prepare   This activity can be done without props. However, gaudy shawls, top hats, military regalia, and articles associated with old-time movie stars would help set the mood. You may want to prepare slips of paper on which you write the names of fictitious "high society" characters, millionaires, movie stars, and others.

Tell the class

You have all been invited to attend a gala ball at the mansion of Mr. and Mrs. Rutherford Upstreet, this city's wealthiest and most aristocratic citizens. Each of you is to attend, not as the person who comes to this class, but as the "high class" people that I know that you really are. Several of you are millionaires, others are movie stars, professional athletes, underworld figures, authors, diplomats, generals, ambassadors, politicians, and play-boys. One of you is a waiter (waitress). Think for a minute about your true identity. Then at the party, introduce yourself to the others, chat, gossip, and even discuss the latest scandals.*

Variation   (*continue*) Just in case you have momentarily forgotten your true identity, I'll remind you of it. I'll give each of you a slip of paper on which is written who you really are.

Check comprehension

Present vocabulary

Reinforce grammar   Rehearse greetings, strategies for interrupting, leave-taking, getting someone's attention, making compliments.

*For English, see page 107; for Spanish, page 121; for French, page 134; for German, page 149.

Ask the class   What questions are you likely to ask at a social event? (Write the questions on the blackboard.)

1. How have you been since I saw you last?
2. What have you been doing lately?
3. Have you seen _____ ?
4. What have you heard about _____ ?
5. Are you related to _____ ?
6. Do you know _____ ?

Divide the class   With smaller classes it may be possible to do this as a whole-class activity. Or, divide the class into groups of about eight students each. If space permits, allow the class to stand and walk around the room as if they were at a party. Remind them of the questions on the blackboard.

Do the activity   You may join as a wealthy guest who knows many of the others. Start rumors and spread gossip. Make sure the student acting as the waiter (or waitress) circulates through the crowd, passing messages from one group to another. The activity can continue for about twenty minutes or until the group tires of it.

In-class discussion topics

1. Why go to formal parties?
2. Are people sincere at parties?
3. How important are the rules of etiquette?
4. Why do people gossip?
5. What makes a scandal?

Follow-up writing topics

1. A party I remember
2. The importance of etiquette
3. Mixing business and pleasure at social gatherings
4. The importance of social status

Use this space for writing in vocabulary

Visitation—*Won't you please come in?*

Objectives

To imagine speaking with an important historical figure
To practice interviewing
To practice politeness and deference

Prepare   No props are required for this activity.

Tell the class

We're going to have some rather unusual visitors today. As some of you know, I have magical powers. I enjoy speaking with ghosts, especially the ghosts of famous people. I've decided to allow you to choose the famous people from the past that you would like to meet. After I bring them here, you, as historians, will have the opportunity to interview them.*

Check comprehension

Present vocabulary

Reinforce grammar   Review ways of making "softened" or polite requests and other ways of showing respect.

Ask the class   What questions would you ask a famous person from the past? (Write the questions on the blackboard.)

1. When did you live?
2. How long did you live?
3. Where did you live?
4. Why do you think you are famous?
5. What do you consider your most important accomplishment?
6. Did you have friends? If so, who were they?
7. Did you have enemies? If so, who were they?
8. Do you have anything to say to the people of today?
9. Will you be remembered two hundred years from now? If so, why?

*For English, see page 107; for Spanish, page 121; for French, page 135; for German, page 149.

Divide the class   Ask the class for suggestions of whom they would like to interview. If their selections are not sufficient, add your own choices, but be sure the students are familiar with the figures you choose. Write the names on the blackboard.

Form groups of three to five students each. Each group chooses the person they want to interview. Have each group choose a secretary. Tell them to write a dialogue. Remind them of the questions on the blackboard.

Do the activity

Call for reports   The groups read aloud their interviews. Encourage other students to ask questions and make comments.

In-class discussion topics

1. Who is your favorite historical figure? Why?
2. Were people "greater" in earlier times?
3. Why is it necessary to study history?
4. Can we really learn from history?

Follow-up writing topics

1. My heroes (heroines) in history
2. The difficulties of doing historical research
3. Effective interview techniques
4. People who say they can communicate with the dead—are they all liars?

Use this space for writing in vocabulary

Honored guest—*Three cheers!*

Objectives

To practice giving short speeches in front of a group
To practice giving praise
To practice the vocabulary of deference

Prepare   No props are required for this activity.

Tell the class

You are needed immediately! The dinner in honor of the president of Zanzania is about to begin. Zanzania is a very controversial country and its president is very unpopular. However, Zanzania is very important to our country, Bartonia. At the last moment, all our business leaders and government officials have refused to attend the dinner. You have been hired to substitute for them. In order to fool the president, you must pretend to be prominent business, government, and military leaders. Each of you must deliver a short speech or toast in honor of the president of Zanzania. I will give you your new identities.*

Check comprehension

Present vocabulary   Practice formal forms of address.

Ask the class   What questions will you have to ask before you write your speech? (Write the questions on the blackboard.)

1. Why am I giving this speech?
2. What can I say to praise the Zanzanian president?
3. How can I show respect for the president even if I don't really mean it?

*For English, see page 107; for Spanish, page 121; for French, page 135; for German, page 150.

Divide the class   Give each student a role to play. Some possible roles are: the head of the Central Bank; the Ministers of education, culture, tourism, and social welfare; the president of the national airline; the head of the federation of athletes; a representative of the international press; and representatives of industries, such as computers, fashion, and automobiles. One student could act as a Zanzanian revolutionary who has infiltrated the dinner party.

Tell them that they will have ten minutes to write a short speech in honor of the president. Remind them of the questions on the blackboard.

Do the activity   Have the students give their toasts. Urge them to stay in character as they speak. Be sure all students have a chance to speak. If you like, play the part of the president of Zanzania. One student may act as master of ceremonies.

In-class discussion topics

1. Why are dinners and receptions held for visiting dignitaries?
2. Why do people make toasts?
3. What are some interesting toasts?
4. What is a good after-dinner speech like?
5. Should protesters be allowed at honorary dinners?

Follow-up writing topics

1. The importance of state visits
2. Making up a toast
3. Planning a dinner in honor of someone
4. The difficulties of being a diplomat

Use this space for writing in vocabulary

Convention—*Let's whoop it up!*

Objectives

To play at being in a secret society or lodge
To devise pranks and secret rituals
To practice greetings

Prepare   No props are required for this activity. Funny or outlandish hats would help establish the desired mood.

Tell the class

Brothers and sisters of the Loyal and Benevolent Order of Rhinoceros, a very secret society, you will all be privileged to attend our national convention. I am sure that all of you, old and new members alike, will have a wild time in the big city. I am sure you will think of new jokes to play and new rituals and traditions.*

Check comprehension

Present vocabulary

Ask the class   What questions do conventioners ask? (Write the questions on the blackboard.)

1. What is your name?
2. Where are you from?
3. Which lodge chapter to you belong to?
4. How long have you been a member?
5. Is this your first convention? What other conventions have you attended?
6. Do you know _____ ?
7. What should we do tonight?
8. How can we have more fun?
9. Can you think of a new ritual for the lodge?

*For English, see page 107; for Spanish, page 122; for French, page 135; for German, page 150.

Divide the class   Tell the class that they are lodge members representing different places. Tell them to decide what kind of member they are. Or, you could assign identities: some could be long-time members or officers, while others are new members. Pranksters, windbags, shy, quiet types and loudmouths should all be represented. The students could act as themselves or take on a different style. Give them a few minutes to think about their roles. With a smaller class, it may be possible to do this as a whole-class activity. Otherwise, divide the class into groups of about eight students each. If space permits, allow the students to walk around the class. Remind them of the questions on the blackboard.

Do the activity   You could join the activity as the lodge's Grand Exalted Leader, the Great Rhinoceros. Or, you could give this honor to one of the students. Encourage the students to be as lively and realistic as they can.

In-class discussion topics
1. Why do people join lodges and secret societies?
2. What do people do in these societies?
3. Why are national conventions held?
4. Have you ever been to a national convention of this type? What was it like?
5. Why do people sometimes act differently at conventions than they do at home?

Follow-up writing topics
1. Lodges and secret societies
2. Conventions
3. My club
4. Rituals, uniforms, and secret sayings
5. Pranks

Use this space for writing in vocabulary

Emergency—*Get help!*

Objectives

To practice reacting to an emergency situation
To practice vocabulary related to rescue and civil defense
To practice command forms and asking factual questions

Prepare   No props are required for this activity.

Tell the class

Disaster has struck! The old dam by the reservoir has broken and the entire area is flooded. Those of you who are members of the rescue team must get to the scene immediately. Others of you have been stranded by the flood waters. Let's get the situation under control as soon as possible!*

Check comprehension

Present vocabulary   Review ways of calling for help and comforting victims.

Ask the class   What questions are asked during an emergency situation? (Write the questions on the blackboard.)

1. What happened?
2. Is anyone hurt? Where? How badly?
3. How much is damaged or lost?
4. What assistance is needed?
5. What has to be done?

*For English, see page 107; for Spanish, page 122; for French, page 136; for German, page 150.

Divide the class   Tell the students to choose a person to portray in the rescue scene. Suggest identities such as: civil defense worker, police chief, fire fighter, mayor, medical aide, national guard member, injured victim, lost child, stranded tourist, elderly person, and a person who has lost a house to the flood. Give them a few minutes to think about their roles. With a smaller class, it may be possible to do this as a whole-class activity. Otherwise, divide the class into groups of about eight students each. If space permits, allow the class to stand and act out their dicussions at the disaster scene. Remind them of the questions on the blackboard.

Do the activity   You may join the activity as a civil defense worker or a flood victim. Encourage the students to be as realistic as possible.

In-class discussion topics

1. Have you ever experienced a natural disaster? What was it like?
2. How do people react to natural disasters?
3. What is the best way to act during a crisis?
4. Who should take command during a disaster situation?
5. Are people sufficiently prepared for disasters?

Follow-up writing topics

1. Managing a crisis
2. Civil defense
3. Preparing for natural disasters
4. Living through disaster

Use this space for writing in vocabulary

APPENDICES

English appendix

Treasures

ancient; artificial; costly; fragile; hard; heavy; round; square; soft; thick

Family portrait

black and white; brave; frightening; funny-looking; handsome; loving; outlaw; photographer; proud; timid

Art critic

artwork; background; bright; calm; critic; intense; masterpiece; to paint; painting; sombre

Flute flight

cheerful; to compose; drums; flute; guitar; harmony; lively; loud; mournful; to play music; soft

Tapestry

to dye; elastic; to reproduce; to sew; soft; stiff; to stretch; to tear; thick; waterproof; to weave

College application

antlers; athlete; bow and arrow; dancer; fin; hooves; intuitive; musician; mysterious; wrestler

Omelet

to boil; to decorate; to dehydrate; to divide; to fry; powdered; to roll; rotten; to scramble; toast

Flim-flam

costume; to deliver; fake; imitation; imposter; invention; loan; to pretend; to promise; uniform

Flagging

arrow; constellation; eagle; eight-sided; rectangular; shield; star; stripe; triangle; to wave

Perfect person

caring; confident; courageous; creative; generous; kind; mature; sense of humor; wealthy; well-built; wise

Recycle

to adapt; to adjust; decoration; to paint; to rebuild; to revolve; useful; useless; to weigh; worn

Dinner party

to bake; bottle; cake; dessert; dinner; food; fresh; to fry; to roast; sour

Vacation

bustling; to camp; to hitchhike; to photograph; to relax; resort; seashore; suntan; tranquil; view

Animal house

antlers; carnivore; herbivore; hoof; mane; neck; paw; tail; trunk; tusk

Student center

auditorium; to chat; gymnasium; locker room; lounge; meeting room; to play; to play cards; swimming pool; tournament

House party

classroom; clinic; dining room; hallway; hostel; kindergarten; kitchen; office; store; theater

Hobby town

antiques; to collect; exciting; to fix; model; to organize; postage stamp; to rebuild; rocket; tropical fish

Chef

to broil; chops; ice cream; layer cake; meat; rice; roast; sauce; to sautée; vegetable; to whip; whipped cream

Floating

to construct; engine; flag; railing; rectangular; round; throne; tilted; tower

Toyland

ball; blocks; box; to hide; to jump; phonograph; playmate; pole; string; to trade

Snake oil

antibiotic; blood pressure; circulation; constipated; dosage; fever; injection; irritation; itching; liquid; pills; prescription

Planning board

air conditioning; cleanup; to clear; to construct; garbage; litter; municipal; ordinance; subway; sound-proof; station

Shipwreck

clothing; to fish; to forage; to gather; hammock; to hunt; primitive; shelter; to weave

Zodiac

carefree; clever; creative; cynical; friendly; industrious; lazy; nurturing; restless; self-confident

Tribal council

to agree; border; camp; cattle; competition; farm; government; industry; property tax

Quick sale

automatic; bag; bargain; camera; cash; cheap; price; ring; ruler; wristwatch

Soft soap

bleach; detergent; filthy; grimy; immaculate; laundry; mop; sponge; spotless; washing machine

Used car

air conditioning; brakes; convertible; engine; heater; hood; horn; miles per hour; speed; tires; windshield

Alma mater

creative; curriculum; extra-curricular; innovative; intensive; leading; practical; preparatory; quality; specialized; technical; vocational

Campaign

brave; conscientious; conservative; honest; leftist; liberal; loyal; platform; reverent; rightist; to run for office; thrifty; trustworthy

Tourist office

casino; cosmopolitan; exclusive; historic; monument; mountainous; picturesque; quaint; relaxing; scenic; stimulating; unspoiled

Mansion

down payment; first class; garage; luxurious; mortgage; to move; neighborhood; orchard; patio; spacious; swimming pool; tennis courts

Air waves

announcer; contest; dial; frequency; improved; jingle; news; sportscaster; sweepstakes

Last rites

assassination; charity; deceased; donation; feared; funeral; heart attack; honored; long illness; religious; revered

Dead language

ally; civilization; culture; diplomacy; diplomat; export; foreign trade; import; literature; tourism; treaty

Taxi driver

bargain; to bargain; festival; monument; museum; passport; plaza; to splurge; stay; to tour

Tour guide

admirable; amusement park; architect; architecture; attraction; cathedral; city hall; exhibition; to inquire; tourist office; unique

Visiting scholar

apartment; dormitory; to enroll; exchange rate; hard-to-find; housing; illegal; major; regulation; required course; transportation; tuition

Nostalgia

to change; coach; failure; memory; nostalgic; successful; to surprise; together; tradition; basketball

High society

boring; elegant; fame; formal; gossip; insult; invitation; to make a toast; rumor; wealthy

Visitation

battle; to conquer; conqueror; discovery; empire; general; to invent; king; scientist; queen

Honored guest

benevolent; brilliant; dedicate; fearless; foresight; greedy; hero; inspiring; leadership; powerful

Convention

to be arrested; to break; drunk; fun; to get drunk; lodge; noisy; old-timer; riotous; silly

Emergency

canned food; dangerous; drinking water; to feed; first aid; help; injured; power boat; to search; stretcher; to treat

Spanish appendix

Treasures

Tengo un problema. Esta mañana caminando a la escuela me encontré con un hombre que llevaba una bolsa grande de papel. Él sacó de la bolsa *este* objeto y me aseguró que tenía muchísimo valor. Sin embargo, como a él le hacía falta dinero, ofreció venderme el objeto por cien dólares solamente. Bueno, yo nunca puedo resistir una ganga, así que se lo compré inmediatamente. Ahora bien, no tengo ninguna seguridad de haber hecho una buena compra, puesto que no tengo ni la más mínima idea de lo que puede ser este objeto. No obstante, como sé que todos Uds. son expertos en antigüedades, por favor, díganme Uds. qué es este objeto y si me engañó o no.

antiguo; artificial; blando; costoso; cuadrado; duro; espeso; frágil; pesado; redondo

Family portrait

Anoche me encontraba en el ático de mi casa y por casualidad levanté la tapa de un baúl que allí estaba arrinconado todo lleno de polvo. Dentro del baúl encontré esta fotografía que Uds. ven aquí. No hay ninguna indicación escrita sobre la foto pero tengo la impresión de que soy de la misma familia de algunas de las personas que en ella aparecen. Sé que todos Uds. son expertos en genealogía y yo he querido mostrarles la foto porque sé que Uds. sabrán decirme quiénes son estas personas y qué hacían en el momento en que les sacaron la foto.

bandido; blanco y negro; cariñoso; curioso; espantoso; fotógrafo; guapo; orgulloso; tímido; valiente

Art critic

Como ya sabrán algunos de Uds., mi querido tío Oscar, fue un famoso coleccionista de arte conocido sobre todo por su afición a coleccionar obras y piezas extrañas, exóticas, y fuera de lo común. Solía decir que dentro de cada obra de arte se escondía un cuento. Pues bien, mi querido tío Oscar se murió el mes pasado y me dejó de herencia algunos de sus objetos preferidos. El problema es que no sé absolutamente nada de arte y me es del todo imposible comprender el significado de los cuadros que me dejó y saber por qué son valiosos. Puesto que sé que Uds. son expertos en la interpretación de obras artísticas y en historia del arte, les ruego que expliquen los cuentos y significados escondidos en estas obras y que juzguen su justo valor y su importancia.

calma; claro, crítico; cuadro; fondo; intenso; obra de arte; obra maestra; pintar; sombrío

Flute flight

El verano pasado mientras viajaba por un lejano país oí una música que en nada se parecía a ninguna que había escuchado hasta ese momento. Su calidad única y especial me intrigó y me cautivó. Por suerte, pude conseguir una grabación de esta música pero no tuve tiempo de enterarme de sus orígenes y significado. Sin embargo, recuerdo haber escuchado que la gente de ese lejano país a menudo emplean su música para relatar cuentos e historias. Todos Uds. son expertos y musicólogos de primer orden. Así que les pido que averigüen los orígenes de esta música y que descubran el cuento que en ella se encierra.

alegre; alto; armonía; componer; enérgico; flauta; guitarra; melancólico; suave; tambores, *m.*; tocar

Tapestry

Traigo conmigo hoy un pedazo de tela muy exótica y fuera de lo común. La fabricaron, usando un proceso secreto, tejedores que vivieron hace muchos años. Que yo sepa, éste es el último pedazo que existe en el mundo. Siempre se ha dicho que esta tela tiene cualidades maravillosas y que es de grandísima utilidad. Me alegro mucho de que Uds. estén aquí hoy. Aquellos de Uds. que son expertos en la manufactura textil tendrán la ocasión de tratar de crear un proceso para reproducir esta tela; los vendedores de tejidos tendrán la oportunidad de formular una lista de los posibles usos de esta tela, mientras que los estudiosos de las religiones del mundo podrán determinar el sistema religioso simbolizado por el diseño de la misma.

coser; duro; elástico; espeso; extender; impermeable al agua; reproducir; romper; suave; tejer; teñir

College application

Acabo de recibir la llamada de la secretaria del comité de admisiones de la Universidad de Heckster. Aparentemente han recibido una solicitud muy fuera de lo común y no saben qué hacer. Quieren ser justos con el solicitante pero hasta la fecha no han visto ningún caso parecido al suyo. Y para complicar y dificultar el asunto aún más, alguien manchó de café una buena parte de la solicitud, volviéndola en gran medida ilegible. Puesto que queda poco tiempo para que se venza el plazo de admisiones, no pueden volver a contactar al solicitante y necesitan descifrar el documento ilegible cuanto antes. Ya que Uds. son muy expertos en materia de culturas extrañas, el comité de admisiones les ruega que hagan el gran favor de tratar de descifrar el contenido de la solicitud. Necesitan saber la identidad del solicitante, así como las razones que da para ser admitido a la Universidad de Heckster. Aquí está la foto que venía adjunta a la solicitud.

aletas; arco y flecha; atleta; bailador; cascos; cornamenta; intuitivo; luchador; misterioso; músico

Character sketch

El editor de este texto ha decidido que la nueva edición que saldrá en un futuro próximo tendrá que incluir una amplia selección de ilustraciones. Está convencido de que incluir ilustraciones de los personajes principales servirá para aumentar la venta del libro. Puesto que todos Uds. son artistas de renombre, han recibido el contrato para ejecutar los dibujos. Fíjense bien que su trabajo refleje exactamente las descripciones que aparecen en el texto.

Omelet

¡Tenemos un problema muy grande, un problema mayúsculo! La computadora ha cometido un error bárbaro. ¡Mañana, a esta misma hora, se entregará a esta misma clase un millón de huevos! Desde luego sería una grandísima pérdida dejar echarse a perder tantos huevos. Ya que Uds. son expertos en el uso y distribución de alimentos, deben planear todas las posibles maneras de usar y distribuir los huevos.

decorar; deshidratar; dividir; en polvo; freír, hacer un revoltillo; hacer rodar; hervir; podrido; tostada

Flim-flam

¡Estoy sin un centavo! Me es del todo imposible sobrevivir con el salario de maestro. Uds. saben lo poquito que reciben los maestros cada dos semanas. Lo que a mí me hace falta es encontrar la manera de volverme rico de la noche a la mañana. Puesto que Uds. son especialistas en asuntos financieros pero a la vez no son del todo honestos en sus operaciones, tuve la idea de que podrían sugerirme la manera de ganar un montón de dinero en poco tiempo. Engañar al público no me causa ningún problema, pero, ¡cuidado! De ningún modo quiero terminar en la cárcel.

disfraz, *m.*; **entregar; falsificación; fingir; imitación; impostor; invención; préstamo; prometer; uniforme**

Flagging

¡Hurra! ¡Viva la República de Bartonia! Bartonia acaba de conseguir su independencia. ¡La gente está bailando por las calles! No obstante, hay un problema difícil de resolver. Los fundadores de Bartonia no han podido ponerse de acuerdo con respecto a la forma, los colores y el diseño de la bandera del nuevo país. El embajador les ruega a Uds., que son expertos en la materia, que inventen y diseñen la nueva bandera. Los colores y el diseño que Uds. elejan, tendrán un significado muy profundo para los ciudadanos de Bartonia.

águila; constelación; escudo; estrella; flecha; octágono; ondear; raya; rectangular; triángulo

Perfect person

A mí me molesta mucho que todas las personas que conozco tengan algún defecto. Ninguna es perfecta. ¡Esta situación me tiene hasta la coronilla! Todas las personas que conozco tienen faltas, debilidades, flaquezas, malos hábitos e imperfecciones. Uds., que son biólogos, ¿pueden resolver mi problema? ¿Pueden diseñarme *la persona perfecta* con todos sus atributos?

bondadoso; cariñoso; confiado; creativo; de buen cuerpo; generoso; maduro; rico; sabio; valiente

Recycle

¡No hay lugar a dudas, se tira a la basura demasiado! El basural de la ciudad está lleno de cosas que podrían usarse otra vez. El alcalde les ha pedido a Uds., los expertos en usar desperdicios, que hagan listas de nuevos usos posibles para las cosas desechadas y desperdiciadas.

adaptar; ajustar; dar vueltas; decoración; inútil; pesar; pintar; reconstruir; usado; útil

Dinner party

Espero que Uds. no se hayan olvidado que tienen seis personas para cenar en su casa (o en su residencia) mañana por la noche. Puesto que no hay mucho tiempo, sería de gran ayuda que seleccionaran el menú usando los productos de una sola tienda. Afortunadamente, los dueños de esta tienda han hecho su publicidad en español. A partir de la información que encuentren en el anuncio, planeen una comida deliciosa para seis invitados. Pueden gastar lo que quieran, pero hagan una lista de sus gastos.

agrio; alimento; asar; botella; comida; freír; fresco; hornear; pastel; postre

Vacation

¡Qué cansancio tengo! Esta clase me tiene con la lengua afuera. Necesito tomar unas vacaciones, pero estoy tan fatigado(a) de trabajar que no tengo bastante energía para planearlas. Puesto que todos Uds. son viajeros expertos y experimentados, les ruego que me hagan el favor de planear mis vacaciones. No me importa cuánto puedan costar. Tengo un presupuesto muy grande.

acampar; animado; costa; descansar; hacer auto-stop; lugar de veraneo; sacar una fotografía; tranquilo; vista

Animal house

Acabo de recibir una llamada telefónica del director de un jardín zoológico no muy lejano de aquí. Me dijo que estaba muy preocupado porque cada día viene menos gente a ver el zoo y porque parece que los animales ya no le interesan a nadie. El director quisiera que Uds. que son biólogos expertos, inventaran un animal completamente nuevo que fuera interesante y atrajera al público. Sería de gran ayuda que Uds. describieran en detalle este nuevo animal en su ambiente natural, lo que come, sus hábitos y costumbres y otras particularidades.

carnívoro; casco; colmillo; cornamenta; crin, _m._; cuello; herbívoro; pata; rabo; trompa

Student center

¡Tengo una gran noticia! ¡No lo van a creer! La administración de la universidad (o de la escuela) les ha elegido para diseñar un nuevo centro estudiantil. Ya que Uds. son arquitectos, han de planear el centro estudiantil más moderno y más completo. Pueden gastar cualquier cantidad de dinero para asegurar que los estudiantes tengan el mejor centro donde divertirse y pasar el rato.

auditorium; campeonato; charlar; gimnasio; jugar; jugar a los naipes; piscina; salón salón social; taquilla

House party

El alcalde de este municipio necesita la ayuda de Uds. Un solterón muy rico acaba de fallecer y ha legado su mansión de diez y ocho habitaciones a la ciudad. El alcalde les pide a Uds. que son muy buenos arquitectos, que hagan una lista de sugerencias de cómo la comunidad podría utilizar esta casa tan grande. Por favor, describan detalladamente su plan preferido.

casa de huéspedes; clínica; cocina; comedor; jardín de infancia; oficina; pasillo; sala de clase; teatro; tienda

Hobby town

¡Que aburrimiento tengo! Mis pasatiempos ya no me llaman la atención y no puedo pensar en nada para pasar las horas libres. Les pido a Uds., expertos en diversiones, entretenimiento y recreación, que me ayuden a planear mi tiempo libre. Deben hacer una lista de actividades que constituyan una verdadera diversión para mí e inventar también un nuevo pasatiempo con el que me aseguren que no voy a aburrirme.

antigüedades; arreglar; cohete, *m.*; coleccionar; emocionante; modelo; organizar; peces tropicales; reconstruir; sellos

Chef

¡Felicitaciones! La Real Academia de Artes Culinarias los ha elegido a Uds. para planear el menú del gran banquete de la graduación de fin de año. Pueden hacer una selección completamente libre de platos e ingredientes. Pueden servir lo que quieran; sin embargo, el banquete tiene que ser extraordinario y presentar un aspecto visual muy interesante. No tengan miedo de inventar nuevas recetas.

arroz; asar a la parrilla; batir; bizcocho de varias camadas, *m.*; carne; carne para asar; crema batida; chuleta; helado; legumbre, *f.*; salsa; saltear

Floating

Me da muchísimo gusto poder anunciar que Uds. han sido elegidos para el diseño y la creación de una carroza que formará parte de la procesión del Día de los Fundadores. El comité de la procesión no ha estipulado ningún límite para la cantidad de dinero que puedan gastar. O sea, tienen mano libre en cuanto a los gastos y materiales para construir la carroza. Más tarde, se juzgarán las carrozas por su belleza y creatividad, por lo tanto, no dejen de crear una carroza muy, muy, pero muy bonita e incluir una descripción detallada y un dibujo de la carroza.

bandera; barandilla; construir; inclinado; motor; rectangular; redondo; torre; trono

Toyland

Mi amigo Ricardo necesita su consejo. Él es un solterón sin hijos y dentro de poco va a recibir la visita de varios de sus sobrinos. Como no posee ningún juguete, ni sabe lo que a los niños les gusta, ni tiene mucho dinero para gastar en juguetes, les pide a Uds. que son expertos en pedagogía, que, por favor, le hagan una lista de juguetes y juegos que sean divertidos, sin peligro y, sobre todo, baratos. Al menos uno de estos juguetes o juegos debe ser de su propia invención.

bloques, *m.*; cajita; cambiar; compañero de juego; cuerdecita; esconderse; palo; pelota; saltar; tocadiscos, *m.*

Snake oil

¡No se imaginan lo difícil que es ser médico hoy en día! ¡Es la cosa más frustrante! Después de tantos años de éxitos y descubrimientos médicos, todavía existen demasiadas enfermedades que los médicos no pueden curar. Lo que necesitamos es una nueva droga milagrosa que sea capaz de curar una enorme cantidad de enfermedades y padecimientos. Por eso, les toca a Uds. que son químicos expertos, descubrir y desarrollar una nueva medicina de este tipo.

antibiótico; circulación; comezón, *f.*; dosis, *f.*; estreñido; fiebre, *f.*; inyección; irritación; líquido; píldoras; presión; receta

Planning board

La situación de la ciudad de Villanueva ha llegado a un estado crítico. Después de años de corrupción en la gobernación, ha tomado las riendas del poder una nueva administración que incluye un nuevo alcalde y nuevos consejales que deben confrontar los múltiples problemas presentes en la ciudad.

Todos Uds. son ayudantes del alcalde y su misión es planear nuevos proyectos que solucionen los problemas de la limpieza, del ruido y del transporte público. Sus ideas deben ser originales e innovadoras. ¡Hagamos de Villanueva una ciudad modelo!

aislado de todo sonido; aire acondicionado; basura; construir; desechos; despejar; estación; limpieza; metro; municipal; ordenanza

Shipwreck

¡Vean ahora si no tenía yo razón! Yo quería volar, tomar el avión, lo que teníamos que haber hecho para llegar a Tahití, pero Uds. insistieron en ir por mar y el barco ha naufragado como consecuencia de una terrible borrasca del Pacífico. ¡Qué suerte que estamos todos sanos y salvos en esta isla desierta que, a pesar de no estar habitada, tiene un clima benigno y una vegetación frondosa! Además tenemos nuestra ropa, fósforos, alambre y unas cuantas medicinas. Tenemos que organizarnos desde ahora mismo y hacer un plan porque puede pasar mucho tiempo antes de que nos vengan a rescatar.

casucha; cazar; coger; forrajear; hamaca; pescar; primitivo; resguardo; ropa; tejer

Zodiac

¡Ha vuelto a ocurrir! El horóscopo ha resultado completamente equivocado. Y como si fuera poco, más y más gente se da cuenta de que su personalidad no encaja para nada en aquéllas que van asociadas con los signos zodiacales como Aries, el carnero; o como Leo, el león. Ya que todos Uds. son astrólogos experimentados, tienen suficiente ciencia para identificar nuevos signos zodiacales y describir las características y personalidad de la gente nacida bajo estos signos.

alimenticio; amistoso; aplicado; cínico; confiado en sí mismo; creativo; despreocupado; intranquilo; listo; perezoso

Tribal council

¡Tengo una noticia terriblemente mala! Como consecuencia de un decreto gubernamental, la tribu a que Uds. pertenecen tiene que abandonar sus tierras ancestrales y ocupar otras. Puesto que Uds. son los ancianos de la tribu, es su responsabilidad preparar a su gente para un cambio drástico y profundo. En el

115

lugar donde van, escasearán todos los recursos, así que el uso y manejo de los mismos determinarán si la tribu podrá prosperar o no. El porvenir de las generaciones futuras está en sus manos.

campamento; competencia; estar de acuerdo; frontera; ganado; gobierno; granja; impuesto; industria; propiedad

Quick sale

¡Tengo una noticia muy urgente! La matrícula de la escuela acaba de subir. Es más, la administración, para evitar problemas burocráticos, exige el pago de la diferencia inmediatamente. Para conseguir este dinero, Uds. tienen que vender algo de lo que llevan encima a sus compañeros de clase. Tendrán que inventar un poco de propaganda para hacerles querer comprar lo que están vendiendo.

anillo; automático; barato; cámara fotográfica; dinero contante; ganga; precio; regla; reloj de pulsera; saco

Soft soap

¡Tenemos suerte! Nuestra compañía de publicidad Fulano y Fulano acaba de conseguir un contrato para trabajar para la compañía de detergentes XYZ. Esta compañía está convencida de que sus productos son mejores y más resistentes que todos los demás que existen en el mercado. Aún mas, tienen poderes extraordinarios. La tarea de Uds. como expertos creadores de publicidad y propaganda, es escribir los avisos publicitarios para la compañía de detergentes XYZ. Tienen que atraer muchísimos nuevos clientes que deseen comprar los productos XYZ.

asqueroso; blanquear; detergente; esponja; inmaculado; lavadora; lavar la ropa; sin mancha; tiznado; trapo

Used car

Tengo un problema. Hace seis meses que trato de vender mi carro pero nadie me lo quiere comprar. Mi carro funciona bien y está en buenas condiciones y el precio que pido es justo; sin embargo todos me dicen que tiene una forma demasiado rara, extraña y diferente y no me lo quieren comprar. ¡Uds. son mi última esperanza! Por favor, como Uds. son especialistas en componer avisos publicitarios y propaganda, escriban un aviso para vender mi carro. Oh, se me olvidó traer una foto del carro pero estoy seguro que Uds. se pueden imaginar la forma de un carro muy poco corriente. Si quieren, pueden tratar de dibujarlo.

aire acondicionado; bocina; capó; calefacción; convertible, *m.*; frenos; gomas; millas por hora; motor; parabrisas, *m.*; velocidad

Alma mater

¡Nuestra querida escuela está pasando por una etapa muy difícil! El número de estudiantes ha disminuido tanto que el año que viene tendrán que cancelarse muchos programas. Si la situación no mejora, dentro de pocos años la escuela tendrá que cerrar sus puertas. Uds. pueden ayudar; Uds. son nuestro último recurso. Puesto que sienten un gran amor por la escuela y conocen todos sus atributos, son las personas más indicadas para escribir anuncios publicitarios a favor de la escuela. Esta publicidad tendrá que atraer a nuevos estudiantes y convencer a los que han dejado la escuela que vuelvan a ella.

calidad; creador; especializado; innovador; intensivo; plan de asignaturas; práctico; preparatorio; principal; profesional; técnico

Campaign

En mi opinión todos los candidatos para las próximas elecciones son malos. Ya no hay ningún gran candidato. Como solución a esta situación, he pensado que Uds. pueden nominar a cualquier persona de hoy en día o del pasado para hacer campaña electoral para las próximas elecciones. Uds. pueden seleccionar a personas de este país o del extranjero. No tienen que ser políticos, ni estar vivos, ni haber existido. Pueden ser bastante originales. Solamente tienen que seleccionar a un candidato, describir cómo es, e inventar y escribir la propaganda política que va a apoyar su candidatura.

concienzudo; confiable; conservador; derechista; económico; honesto; izquierdista; leal; liberal; presentarse; programa; reverente; valiente

Tourist office

Tengo muchísimo gusto en darles la bienvenida a todos Uds. a este gran simposio celebrado aquí en Las Naciones Unidas como el acto cumbre que finaliza el "Año del Turista." Uds., representantes de sus respectivos países, saben que el constante aumento del costo de viajes amenaza el futuro de la industria turística a escala mundial y la economía de los países que de ella dependen. Parte de su labor como conferenciantes y asistentes al simposio, será la formulación y elaboración de descripciones detalladas de los atractivos y posibilidades de una eficaz explotación turística de sus países.

Los representantes de Ricolandia, Mediolandia y Pobrelandia se reunirán por separado para preparar sus materiales. Después tendremos ocasión de juntarnos todos y compartir las ideas.

casino; cosmopolita; estimulante; exclusivo; histórico; montañoso; monumento; panorámico; pintoresco; sin estropear; singular

Mansion

¡No lo comprendo! Ya hace meses que estas casas tan bonitas están en venta y nadie las compra. Los agentes de bienes raíces no se lo explican y están muy frustrados. Ellos les piden a Uds., que son expertos en la materia, que tengan la amabilidad de darles una mano y escribir avisos publicitarios que atraigan compradores. Si las casas se llegan a vender, Uds. pueden contar con una buena comisión.

espacioso; garaje; huerta; hipoteca; lujoso; patio; piscina; pista de tenis; primera clase; trasladarse; vecindad

Air waves

Los dueños de la estación de radio WXXX están muy preocupados. Tienen cada vez menos oyentes para sus programas. A menos que esta situación cambie de manera radical, tendrá que cerrarse la emisora. Solamente Uds., asesores de primer orden, están capacitados para dar nueva vida a la estación WXXX mediante la creación de publicidad para la radio que atraiga a nuevos oyentes y aumente rápidamente el número de ellos. Uds. pueden también inventar juegos y competencias originales para la radio y sugerir una programación más variada e interesante. ¡Salvemos la emisora WXXX!

anunciador de deportes; anuncio rimado; banda; concurso; frecuencia; locutor; lotería; mejorado; noticias

Last rites

¡Traigo muy malas noticias! Varias personalidades de renombre internacional han muerto recientemente de manera repentina. Entre ellas se encuentran el Honorable Alfonso Saltacolinas, ex-embajador de la República de Wellingtonia a los E.E.U.U., Max "el Mosca" Jones, el infame asesino, ladrón de joyas y hampón de larga y escalofriante reputación, y, por último, Doña Edith Dísono, conocida soprano de la Ópera de Oeste. Sin embargo, estos fallecimientos no pasarán inadvertidos. Eso lo pueden dar por seguro. Como hábiles periodistas, Uds. tienen el honor de escribir los obituarios de estas personas tan importantes.

asesinato; ataque de corazón; caridad; difunto; donación; funeral; larga enfermedad; religioso; temible; venerado

Dead language

Acabo de recibir noticias desconcertantes. Las inscripciones para los cursos de hondari, la lengua de Hondaristán, han disminuido drásticamente. Esta lengua, tan estudiada en un pasado reciente, ha perdido su popularidad entre los estudiantes. La administración está a punto de cancelar todo el programa de hondari. Es por eso que el jefe del departamento de lenguas modernas les ha pedido a Uds., que son peritos en muchas lenguas, que por favor, le escriban una carta urgentemente a la administración explicando por qué la enseñanza de hondari debería continuarse y sugiriendo diferentes maneras de atraer a estudiantes a los cursos de hondari.

aliado; civilización; comercio extranjero; cultura; diplomacia; diplomático; exportación; importación; literatura; tratado; turismo

Taxi driver

Después de siete interminables horas de vuelo, Ud. llega por fin a la ciudad de Wallen, la capital de Contursia. Con un poco de suerte Ud. encuentra un taxi, pero está un poco nervioso porque no habla ni una palabra de contursi y el chofer del taxi parece ignorar la lengua materna de Ud. Sin embargo, pronto Ud. descubre que el chofer está aprendiendo español y sabe tanto de esa lengua extranjera como Ud., más o menos. Como el viaje es largo desde el aeropuerto hasta la ciudad, tienen tiempo de sobra para hablar y conocerse.

estadía; fachendear; ganga; monumento; museo; pasaporte; plaza; regatear; viajar

Tour guide

Tengo que pedirles un favor. Mi tío va a venir a pasar algún tiempo aquí para visitar el área. Será su primera visita aquí y quiere ver todos los puntos de interés. Desafortunadamente, dispongo de muy poco tiempo libre la semana próxima. Es más, no conozco bien la región. Puesto que Uds. son guías turísticos muy experimentados, pueden planear la visita de mi tío. Les estaré muy agradecido(a).

admirable; arquitecto; arquitectura; averiguar; catedral, *f.*; diversión; exposición; oficina de turismo; parque de diversiones; único

Visiting scholar

¡Traigo noticias estupendas! Todos Uds. han ganado una beca para pasar un año en un país donde se habla español. Tienen que hablar solamente español durante todo el año. Éste es el único requisito. Ya que va a ser algo difícil hacerlo, sería una buena idea formar grupos para ayudarse mutuamente, encontrarse, y practicar antes de hacer el viaje hacia el nuevo país. Dentro de estos grupos, Uds. pueden discutir cómo solucionar los problemas de vivienda, de traslado dentro del país, de comida extraña, de contacto con la gente y del procedimiento para inscribirse en la universidad. No hay tiempo que perder. Deben empezar a prepararse inmediatamente.

alojamiento; apartamento; cambio; difícil de encontrar; especialización; ilegal; inscribirse; matrícula; regulación; requisito; residencia estudiantil; transporte, *m.*

Nostalgia

Todos Uds. han tenido el privilegio de ser invitados a la vigésima quinta reunión de la clase de 19 – – del Colegio Jazmín. Puesto que todos Uds. fueron condiscípulos, seguramente tendrán muchísmo gusto en volverse a encontrar y en hablar de su vida y de los cambios que han ocurrido a lo largo de los últimos veinticinco años. Traten de acordarse de los chismes de hace veinticinco años.

Variante (*continuando*) Puesto que soy yo la única persona que los conocía a Uds. entonces y los conoce ahora, les recordaré quiénes son y quiénes fueron: La reina del baile de fin de año; el atleta héroe de fútbol; el presidente de la clase; la tímida que se hizo estrella de cine; el valentón ahora jefe de policía; el "profe" de inglés ya entrado en años que de todos se acuerda; la estrella de la obra teatral del final de curso; el entrenador jubilado; los aficionados fanáticos que no perdían ni un partido y los tipos corrientes que no ponían ni quitaban.

balconcesto; cambiar; con éxito; entrenador; fracaso; juntos; memoria; nostálgico; sorprender; tradición

High society

Todos Uds. han sido invitados a asistir al baile de gala en la mansión de los Sres. Callearriba, los ciudadanos más ricos y aristocráticos de nuestra ciudad. Cada uno de Uds. asistirá en calidad de persona de la alta sociedad a la que de hecho pertenece. Varios entre Uds. son millonarios; otros estrellas de cine, atletas profesionales, magnates del mundo criminal, autores célebres, diplomáticos, generales, embajadores, políticos y casanovas de reputación muy amplia. Uno de Uds. es camarero. Piensen en su identidad y durante el baile, preséntense los unos a los otros, pónganse a charlar, a contar chismes y a opinar sobre los más recientes escándalos.

Variante (*continuando*) Por si acaso se les olvida momentáneamente su verdadera identidad yo se la recordaré. Le daré a cada uno un papelito que llevará escrita su identidad real.

aburrido; adinerado; brindar; chisme, *m.*; elegante; fama, *f.*; formal; insulto; invitación; rumor

Visitation

Hoy vamos a tener el gusto de recibir la visita de algunos personajes muy poco comunes. Como Uds. saben, yo tengo poderes mágicos. Me gusta pasar tiempo conversando con fantasmas, sobre todo con los fantasmas de personalidades famosas. He decidido dejarles a Uds. elegir a las personas famosas del pasado con quienes Uds. quisieran hablar. Después de que aparezcan aquí entre nosotros, Uds., en su capacidad de historiadores, tendrán la oportunidad de hacerles una entrevista.

batalla; científico; conquistador; conquistar; descubrimiento; general; imperio; inventar; reina; rey

Honored guest

¡Se requiere urgentemente su presencia! La cena en honor del presidente de Zanzania está a punto de comenzar. Deben saber que Zanzania es un país que ha suscitado mucha controversia y su presidente no es nada popular. No obstante, en el actual escenario político, Zanzania desempeña un papel crítico para con nuestro país Bartonia, y es de suma importancia que se mantengan relaciones amistosas entre los dos países. Sin embargo, a última hora, los miembros de nuestro gobierno y líderes del sector industrial de nuestro país han rehusado asistir a esta cena de gala en honor del presidente. Así es que se ha pensado que Uds. tienen que sustituir a las personas que se han negado a venir a la cena. Y para engañar bien al presidente de Zanzania, tienen que fingir que son esos hombres y mujeres de negocios, esos miembros del gobierno. Cada uno de Uds. tendrá que dar un pequeño discurso o brindis en honor a nuestro ilustre invitado, el presidente de Zanzania. Claro que para hacer estos papeles tendrán que recibir nuevas identidades.

benévolo; brillante; codicioso; dedicado; dotes de mando, *m.*; héroe; inspirante; intrépido; poderoso; previsión

Convention

Mis queridos y queridas hermanos y hermanas de la más leal y benevolente Orden del Rinoceronte: tengo el gran honor, gusto, y privilegio de poder anunciarles que en un futuro muy próximo se llevará a cabo la celebración de nuestra convención nacional a la que, sobra decirlo, están desde este momento invitados. Esperamos este año la concurrencia de toda la gran familia que forman nuestros miembros, tantos viejos como jóvenes, y que la diversión, gozo, y júbilo este año alcancen cimas más altas y rompan barreras nuevas. Estamos seguros de que la inspiración e imaginación no les faltarán para inventar bromas nuevas y rituales originales.

alborotado; borracho; diversión; emborracharse; logia; ridículo; romper; ruidoso; ser detenido; veterano

Emergency

¡Terrible catástrofe! El antiguo dique del embalse acaba de romperse y se ha inundado una buena parte de la región. Los miembros del equipo de rescate deben presentarse inmediatamente en el lugar del siniestro. Los demás se encuentran en situación precaria, completamente aislados y rodeados de las aguas turbias de la inundación. ¡Vamos a ver si conseguimos poner la situación bajo control cuanto antes!

agua potable; alimentar; autobote, *m.*; ayuda; buscar; camilla; comida enlatada; lesionado; peligroso; primeros auxilios; tratar

French appendix

Treasures

Je ne comprends pas! Ce matin j'allais à l'école. Un monsieur m'a arrêté(e). Il portait un grand sac en papier. Regardez! Il a sorti cet objet du sac. Il m'a dit qu'il était d'une très grande valeur. Ce monsieur avait vraiment besoin d'argent. Il a voulu me vendre "ceci" pour $100. C'est tout! Moi, j'adore les bonnes affaires, alors je l'ai acheté tout de suite. Maintenant, je me pose des questions. Je ne sais même pas ce que j'ai acheté. Mais vous êtes tous experts en antiquités. Pouvez-vous m'expliquer ce que c'est? Dites-moi aussi si je me suis fait avoir.

ancien; artificiel; carré; coûteux; dur; épais; fragile; lourd; mou; rond

Family portrait

Hier soir, j'étais au grenier. J'ai ouvert une vieille malle qui était couverte de poussière. Au fond de cette malle, j'ai trouvé cette photo. Il n'y a aucune inscription dessus mais elle représente, me semble-t-il, quelques-uns de mes ancêtres. Je sais que vous êtes très forts en généalogie, alors regardez! Dites-moi qui sont ces gens et ce qu'ils faisaient quand cette photo a été prise.

affectueux; beau; bizarre; courageux; effrayant; hors-la-loi, *m.*; noir et blanc; orgueilleux; photographe, *m.*; timide

Art critic

Comme vous le savez puet-être, mon cher oncle Oscar était collectionneur d'art. Il était connu pour ses goûts bizarres évidents dans son choix d'oeuvres étranges. Il disait, mon oncle, que derrière chaque oeuvre se cachait une histoire. Mon oncle est mort il y a un mois et il m'a laissé certains de ses objets préférés. Mais je ne connais rien à l'art. Je ne sais pas ce que veulent dire les tableaux ou pourquoi ils ont de la valeur. A vous, experts en interprétation de l'art, de m'expliquer les secrets de ces oeuvres et d'évaluer leur importance dans le monde de l'art.

arriè-plan, *m.*; brillant; calme; chef-d'oeuvre, *m.*; critique, *m.*; intense; oeuvre d'art, *f.*; sombre; tableau, *m.*

Flute flight

L'été dernier, j'étais à l'étranger. Un jour, j'ai entendu une musique mystérieuse qui ne ressemblait à aucune autre que j'avais entendue auparavant. J'étais surpris(e) par ses qualités merveilleuses. J'ai pu acheter un enregistrement de cette musique mais j'étais pressé(e) et je n'ai pas eu le temps de demander des précisions sur l'origine et sur la signification de cette musique. Tout ce que je sais, c'est que les habitants de cette région se servent souvent de musique pour raconter une histoire. Vous qui êtes musicologues, écoutez et dites-moi l'origine et la signification de cette musique.

batterie, *f.*; composer; doux; faire de la musique; flûte, *f.*; fort; guitare, *f.*; harmonie, *f.*; lugubre; vif

Tapestry

Aujourd'hui j'ai sur moi un morceau de tissu très spécial. Il a été fabriqué selon un procédé secret par des tisseurs qui sont morts depuis bien longtemps. A ma connaissance ceci est le seul morceau qui en reste au monde! Ce tissu a beaucoup de propriétés merveilleuses et l'on peut l'utiliser pour beaucoup de choses. A vous les fabricants de reproduire ce tissu. A vous les commerçants d'énumérer les utilisations possibles de ce tissu. A vous les experts en religions du monde de nous expliquer les mystères religieux associés avec les dessins répétés sur ce tissu.

coudre; déchirer; élastique; épais; imperméable; mou; rêche; reproduire; teindre; tendre; tisser

College application

La secrétaire du comité d'inscriptions de l'Université de Heckster vient d'appeler. Elle a reçu une demande d'inscription qui est très étrange. Personne ne sait quoi en faire. La photo qui est jointe à l'inscription montre quelqu'un de très bizarre. De plus, on a renversé du café sur cette demande et on ne peut presque plus lire ce qui est marqué dessus. Il n'y a pas de temps pour contacter cette personne pour redemander des renseignements. Alors on vous demande en tant qu'experts ethnologues de déterminer ce qui aurait pu être marqué sur la demande. Etudiez cette photo et essayez de voir qui est cet individu. Surtout essayez de déterminer s'il faut l'accepter à l'université.

arc, *m.*; et des flèches, *f. pl.*; athlète, *m., f.*; bois, *m.*; danseur, *m.*; intuitif; lutteur, *m.*; musicien, *m.*; mystérieux; nageoire, *f.*; sabots, *m. pl.*

Character sketch

L'éditeur de ces livres a décidé qu'il fallait y ajouter des illustrations pour la nouvelle édition. Il pense que des portraits des personnages principaux sont nécessaires pour mieux vendre les livres. Vous, qui êtes des artistes très connus, avez reçu le contrat pour faire ces portraits. Mais surtout dessinez-les exactement selon les descriptions des personnages qui se trouvent dans le texte.

Omelet

Nous avons un problème, les ordinateurs ont fait erreur. Demain, à cette heure-ci on va nous livrer un milliard d'oeufs—ici dans cette salle de classe! Qu'est-ce que nous pourrons en faire? C'est bête de les gaspiller. En tant qu'experts en alimentation, pensez à comment on pourrait utiliser et distribuer des oeufs!

bouillir; brouiller; décorer; déshydrater; diviser; en poudre; frire; pain grillé, _m._; pourri; rouler

Flim-flam

Je suis vraiment fâché(e). Je n'arrive pas à joindre les deux bouts avec mon salaire de professeur. Vous savez, les professeurs gagnent très peu d'argent. Ce qu'il me faudrait, c'est une méthode infaillible pour me faire beaucoup d'argent très vite! Vous, qui êtes des hommes et des femmes d'affaires peu scrupuleux, vous pouvez me dire comment me procurer beaucoup d'argent en peu de temps. Tromper le public est tout à fait acceptable pour moi. Mais attention! Je ne veux pas aller en prison!

déguisement, _m._; faire semblant; faux, _m._; emprunt, _m._; imitation, _f._; imposteur, _m._; invention, _f._; livrer; promettre; uniforme, _m._

Flagging

Hourra! Vive la République de Bartonie! Elle vient de recevoir son indépendance. On danse dans les rues. Maintenant il faut un drapeau à ce nouveau pays. Alors l'ambassadeur de la Bartonie vous demande, en tant que fabricants de drapeaux, de leur créer un drapeau qui fera le bonheur de tous les Bartoniens. Il faut être prêts à expliquer vos choix de couleurs et de motifs. Si vous avez le temps, vous pouvez également créer une devise pour eux.

aigle, _m._; bouclier, _m._; constellation, _f._; flèche, _f._; flotter; étoile, _f._; octogonal; rayure, _f._; rectangulaire; triangle, _m._

Perfect person

Il me semble que chaque personne que je rencontre a des défauts. J'en ai assez! Tout le monde a des faiblesses, de mauvaises habitudes—bref, des imperfections de quelque sorte. A vous, biologistes, de me créer *la personne parfaite.*

aimable; bien fait; créateur; courageux; généreux; prévenant; riche; sage; sens de l'humour, *m.*; sûr(e) de lui (d'elle)

Recycle

Il y a trop de gaspillage! La décharge municipale est remplie d'objets que l'on pourrait réutiliser. Le maire de notre ville vous demande, en tant qu'experts en recyclage, de bien vouloir enumérer de nouvelles utilisations pour vieux objets.

adapter; ajuster; décoration, *f.*; inutile; peindre; peser; reconstruire; tourner; usé; utile

Dinner party

J'espère que vous n'avez pas oublié qu'il y aura six personnes à dîner chez vous demain soir. Etant donné que vous n'aurez pas beaucoup de temps pour faire les courses, vous ferez mieux de les faire dans un seul magasin.

Regardez—nous avons des circulaires en français! Quelle chance! Alors, pensez à un repas délicieux, en vous servant de ce qui est en réclame. Vous pouvez dépenser autant d'argent que vous voulez, mais il faut noter vos dépenses.

aigre; bouteille, *m.*; cuire; dessert, *m.*; dîner, *m.*; frais; frire; gâteau, *f.*; nourriture, *m.*; rôtir

Vacation

Je suis exténué(e), épuisé(e). J'ai besoin de vacances, mais je suis tellement fatigué(e) que je ne peux même pas réfléchir à où il faudrait aller. Vous qui êtes voyageurs passionnés et qui connaissez tant de pays, choisissez et préparez mon voyage. Le prix m'est égal!

affairé; bord de la mer, *m.*; se bronzer; faire du camping; faire du stop; lieu de séjour, *m.*; prendre une photo; se reposer; tranquille; vue, *f.*

Animal house

Je viens de recevoir un coup de fil du directeur du jardin zoologique régional. Il est très inquiet parce qu'il y a de moins en moins de gens qui visitent le zoo. Il faut croire que le public ne s'intéresse plus aux animaux. A vous, les biologistes, d'inventer un nouvel animal qui attirera de nouveau le public au zoo. Décrivez cet animal—décrivez également son habitat, sa nourriture, ses habitudes, et d'autres détails qui pourraient être utiles.

bois, *m. pl.*; carnivore; crinière, *f.*; cou, *m.*; défense, *f.*; herbivore; patte, *f.*; queue, *f.*; sabot, *m.*; trompe, *f.*

Student center

J'ai des nouvelles formidables! Les membres du conseil d'éducation vous ont choisis pour dessiner les plans du nouveau centre d'étudiants. En tant qu'architectes et dessinateurs, vous devez créer un centre qui soit à la fois complet et ultramoderne. Vous pouvez dépenser autant que vous voulez. Donnez aux étudiants un centre unique au monde!

bavarder; causer; foyer, *m.*; gymnase, *m.*; jouer; jouer aux cartes; piscine, *f.*; salle de conférences, *f.*; tournoi, *m.*; vestiaire, *m.*

House party

Le maire a besoin de votre aide. Un vieux célibataire très riche vient de mourir. Il a légué à la ville sa maison de dix-huit pièces. Le maire donc demande à vous, architectes, d'énumérer toutes les utilisations possibles de cette maison et ensuite de décrire en détail le plan que vous préférez.

auberge de jeunesse, *f.*; bureau, *m.*; clinique, *f.*; cuisine, *f.*; jardin d'enfants, *m.*; magasin, *m.*; salle à manger, *f.*; salle de classe, *f.*; théâtre, *m.*; vestibule, *m.*

Hobby town

Je m'ennuie! Mes vieux passe-temps favoris ne m'intéressent plus! Je ne sais plus quoi faire pendant mon temps libre. Mais vous, les experts en loisirs, pouvez-vous me faire des suggestions? Décrivez-moi les activités qui me plairont. Ensuite, inventez un nouveau passe-temps qui soit garanti de ne pas m'ennuyer.

antiquité, *f.*; collectionner; excitant; fusée, *f.*; modèle, *m.*; organiser; poisson tropical, *m.*; reconstruire, *f.*; réparer; représentation, *f.*; timbre-poste, *m.*

Chef

Félicitations! L'Académie de la Haute Cuisine vous a choisis pour vos talents de maîtres-cuisiniers pour décider le menu de leur banquet des diplômés. Vous avez libre choix quant aux ingrédients. Choisissez ce que vous voulez. Faites un menu varié, intéressant, et surtout très original. N'ayez pas peur d'inventer de nouveaux plats!

battre; côtelette, *f.*; crème fouettée; gâteau, *m.*; glace, *f.*; griller, légume, *m.*; riz, *m.*; rôti, *m.*; sauce, *f.*; sauter; viande, *f.*

Floating

C'est formidable! Cette classe a été choisie pour dessiner un char pour le défilé du jour de la commémoration. La comité du défilé vous permet de dépenser autant d'argent que vous voulez pour les matériaux. Les chars seront jugés par un groupe d'experts en fonction de leur beauté et de leur originalité. Vous devez décrire votre char et en faire un dessin.

construire; drapeau, *m.*; garde-fou, *m.*; moteur, *m.*; penché; rectangulaire; rond; tour, *f.*; trône, *m.*

Toyland

Mon ami, Richard, qui est célibataire, a besoin de vos conseils. Ses petits neveux et nièces vont venir chez lui pendant un bout de temps. Le problème, c'est que Richard ne connaît rien aux enfants et en plus, il n'a pas un seul jouet chez lui! Il voudrait bien en acheter, mais non seulement il n'a pas beaucoup d'argent, il n'a aucune idée des jouets qui feraient plaisir aux enfants. Pouvez-vous, vous qui êtes experts en jeux éducatifs, décrire des jeux et des jouets qui soient à la fois divertissants, sans danger et de plus, bon marché? Il faut qu'au moins un des articles soit de votre propre invention.

ballon, *m.*; bâton, *m.*; boîte, *m.*; se cacher; copain, *m.*; cube, *m.*; échanger; ficelle, *f.*; sauter; tourne-disque, *m.*

Snake oil

C'est dur d'être médecin de nous jours. C'est frustrant. Après tant d'années de recherches et de découvertes en médecine, il y a quand même encore beaucoup de maladies inguérissables. Il faudrait un nouveau médicament-miracle. A vous, chimistes experts, de développer un nouveau médicament qui pourrait guérir une multitude de maladies.

antibiotique, *m.*; cachet, *m.*; circulation, *f.*; constipé; démangeaison, *f.*; dose, *f.*; fièvre, *f.*; injection, *f.*; irritation, *f.*; ordonnance, *f.*; tension artérielle, *f.*

Planning board

La ville de Centrebourg est une honte! Des années de mauvaise gérance de la part du maire et des conseillers municipaux ont fait de notre ville une poubelle géante! Mais la nouvelle administration qui s'intéresse à faire des réformes vient de vous choisir comme membres du conseil administratif. Il y a plusieurs projets importants qu'il faut commencer tout de suite—c'est à dire un nettoyage total de la ville, un programme de réduction du bruit ambiant et la construction d'un système de transports rapides. Soyez innovateurs et originaux avec les projets! Faites de Centrebourg une ville modèle!

climatisation, *f.*; construire; déblayer; détritus, *m. pl.*; insonorisé; métro, *m.*; municipal; ordonnance, *f.*; ordures, *f. pl.*; station, *f.*

Shipwreck

J'avais raison! Je voulais prendre l'avion mais vous avez insisté sur le bateau pour aller à Tahiti. Et voilà! Le bateau coule pendant un orage tropical. Nous avons de la chance d'être toujours en vie! Nous voici maintenant sur cette île déserte. Le climat est agréable et il y a beaucoup de végétation. Nous sommes seuls ici. Nous n'avons pas grand'chose—à part quelques allumettes, quelques couteaux, un peu de fil de fer, quelques médicaments, et les vêtements que nous avons sur nous. Il faut s'organiser et faire des plans. Qui sait quand on viendra nous sauver?

abri, *m.*; cabane, *f.*; chasser; cueillir; fourrager; hamac, *m.*; pêcher; primitif; tisser; vêtements, *m. pl.*

Zodiac

Encore une fois—un horoscope s'est trompé. Et puis, de plus en plus de gens prétendent que leur personnalité diffère énormément des descriptions des personnalités associées avec chaque signe du Zodiaque. Par exemple, le bélier, Aries—ou bien le lion, Leo. A vous, astrologues experts, de nous aider. A vous d'identifier de nouveaux signes astrologiques qui correspondraient mieux aux traits de caractère de ceux qui sont nés sous chaque signe.

agité; amical; créateur; cynique; diligent; paresseux; protecteur; sans souci; sûr(e) de soi

Tribal council

J'ai des nouvelles épouvantables! Une décision gouvernementale vient d'être prise, qui vous enlèvera vos terres. Vous vivez ici depuis des siècles, mais maintenant il faut aller vivre dans une autre région. En tant qu'anciens de la tribu, vous devez préparer votre peuple pour ce changement profond dans votre train de vie. Les ressources y sont limitées. Les décisions que vous prenez aujourd'hui sont d'une importance primordiale. Leurs conséquences seront ressenties par des générations à venir.

bétail, *m.*; camp, *m.*; concurrence, *f.*; consentir; ferme, *f.*; frontière, *f.*; gouvernement, *m.*; impôt, *m.*; industrie; propriété

Quick sale

J'ai des nouvelles urgentes! L'administration vient d'augmenter vos frais de scolarité. Chacun de vous doit payer la différence tout de suite. Vous devez choisir quelque chose que vous avez sur vous, et le vendre à un de vos camarades de classe. Vous devez aussi préparer une campagne publicitaire pour mieux le vendre.

appareil photographique, *m.*; argent comptant, *m.*; automatique; bague, *f.*; bon marché; montre-bracelet, *m.*; occasion, *f.*; prix, *m.*; règle, *m.*; sac, *m.*

Soft soap

Quelle chance! Notre agence de publicité, Lavant, Laver et Laverons, vient d'être engagée par la compagnie de lessive Sipropre. Cette compagnie insiste sur le fait que son produit est le meilleur au monde, qu'il a des pouvoirs extraordinaires! A vous, écrivains de publicité, de créer des réclames pour ce produit de lessive qui attireront beaucoup de nouveaux clients.

blanchir; crasseux; dégoûtant; éponge, *f.*; impeccable; lessive, *f.*; machine à laver, *f.*; sale

Used car

J'ai un problème. Cela fait déjà six mois que j'essaye de vendre ma voiture, mais personne ne veut l'acheter. Elle marche bien et le prix est raisonnable mais tout le monde me dit que ma voiture est trop bizarre. Vous êtes mon dernier espoir! En tant que spécialistes en publicité, vous devez composer une annonce qui m'assure la vente de ma voiture. Je n'ai pas de photo d'elle sur moi, mais vous pouvez imaginer à quoi elle ressemble. Si vous voulez, vous pouvez même en faire un dessin.

capot, *m.*; chauffage, *m.*; climatisation, *f.*; décapotable, *f.*; freins, *m.*; kilomètres-heure, *m.*; klaxon, *m.*; moteur, *m.*; pare-brise, *m.*; pneu, *m.*; vitesse, *f.*

Alma mater

Notre chère école est menacée par un manque d'étudiants! On doit annuler beaucoup de programmes prévus pour l'année prochaine et si cette tendance continue, il faudra éventuellement fermer l'école complètement. Vous qui aimez cette école, aidez-la! Vous devez refaire la publicité de l'école pour attirer de nouveaux étudiants et pour convaincre ceux qui sont déjà partis d'y revenir.

créateur; innovateur; intensif; plan de'études, *m.*; pratique; premier; préparatoire; professionnel; qualité, *f.*; spécialisé; technique

Campaign

Je n'aime pas les candidats qui se présentent aux prochaines élections. Je dirais même qu'il n'y a plus jamais de bons candidats. A vous de désigner quelqu'un qui, à votre avis, serait un bon choix. Vous pouvez choisir quelqu'un de réel ou d'imaginaire, de vivant ou de mort, de profession politique ou autre, de votre pays ou de l'étranger—comme vous voulez. Choisissez votre candidat et ensuite préparez sa campagne électorale, en incluant des slogans et de la littérature qui parle de lui.

consciencieux; conservateur; courageux; de droite; de gauche; digne de confiance; économe; honnête; libéral; loyal; se présenter; programme, *m.*; respectueux

Tourist office

Mes chers collègues, en tant que représentants des Ministères du Tourisme de vos pays, vous êtes les bienvenus à cette conférence des Nations Unies qui honore l'Année du Touriste. Comme vous le savez, l'augmentation du prix des voyages menace l'avenir de votre industrie et de l'économie de chacun de vos pays. Au cours de cette conférence vous allez formuler des descriptions nouvelles et persuasives des vertus de vos pays—ceci dans le but d'amener plus de touristes chez vous.

Les représentants de la Terreriche, de la Terremoyenne, et de la Terrepauvre se réuniront séparément pour préparer leurs matériaux. Nous nous retrouverons plus tard pour mesurer ensemble l'efficacité de vos projets, en les essayant les uns sur les autres.

casino, *m.*; cosmopolite; exclusif; historique; montagneux; monument, *m.*; non souillé; pittoresque; reposant; stimulant; typique

Mansion

Je ne comprends pas. Ces villas magnifiques sont à vendre depuis des mois, mais personne ne veut les acheter. Les agents immobiliers son frustrés. Ils vous demandent en tant qu'experts en immobilier d'écrire une annonce qui attirera des acheteurs. Si les villas sont vendues, vous recevrez une belle prime!

apport personnel; court de tennis, *m.*; de premier ordre; déménager; garage, *m.*; hypothèque, *f.*; luxueux; piscine, *f.*; quartier, *m.*; somptueux; spacieux; verger, *m.*

Air waves

Les propriétaires de la station de radio WXXX sont très inquiets. Il y a de moins en moins d'auditeurs—au point où il faudrait peut-être bientôt fermer la station. En tant que consultants experts, vous pouver sauver la station. Vous devez écrire de la publicité pour radio qui attirera des auditeurs. Vous devez également inventer des jeux et des concours à radio-diffuser, ainsi que suggérer de nouveaux programmes. Sauvons Radio WXXX!

cadran, *m.*; commentateur de sports, *m.*; concours, *f.*; enjeu, *m.*; fréquence, *f.*; indicatif, *m.*; nouvelles, *f.*; perfectionné; speaker, *m.*; speakerine, *f.*

Last rites

J'ai une triste nouvelle à vous annoncer. Plusieurs personnages qui sont connus mondialement sont morts—tous à la fois: l'honorable Alphonse Muggeridge, ancien ambassadeur de Wellingtonia aux Etats-Unis; Max "La Mouche" Jones, le meurtrier infâme, voleur de bijoux et membre d'une bande internationale; et puis Dame Edith Chante-Bien, prima donna de la Compagnie d'Opéra Occidentale. Mais ces morts ne passeront pas inaperçues. A vous, journalistes habiles d'écrire la nécrologie de ces personnages importants!

assassinat, *m.*; charité, *f.*; crise cardiaque, *f.*; défunt; donation, *f.*; enterrement, *m.*; honoré; maladie prolongée, *f.*; religieux; vénéré

Dead language

Je viens de recevoir des nouvelles inquiétantes. Il y a une baisse considérable du nombre de demandes d'inscription pour les cours de hondari, la langue du Hondaristan. Les étudiants ne s'intéressent plus à cette langue qui était si appréciée auparavant. En conséquence, l'administration de l'école menace d'annuler tout le programme de hondari. Alors le chef du département des langues étrangères vous demande, à vous qui vous consacrez aux langues, d'écrire à l'administration. Dans votre lettre vous devez expliquer pourqoui il ne faut pas annuler le programme de hondari. De plus, vous devez suggérer un plan pour attirer plus d'étudiants à l'étude de cette langue.

affaires étrangères, *f.*; allié; civilisation, *f.*; culture, *f.*; diplomate, *m.*; diplomatie, *m.*; exportation, *f.*; importation, *f.*; littérature, *f.*; tourisme, *m.*; traité, *m.*

Taxi driver

Après un vol fatigant qui a duré sept heures, vous êtes enfin arrivé(s) à Wallen, la capitale de la Contursia. Quelle chance! Vous trouvez un taxi tout de suite. Mais il y a un petit problème. Vous ne parlez pas contursien et le chauffeur du taxi ne parle pas votre langue. Mais vous remarquez tout de suite que le chauffeur lui aussi est en train d'étudier le français et qu'il le sait aussi bien que vous. Le trajet de l'aéroport au centre ville est long. Vous aurez beaucoup de temps pour vous parler et pour faire connaissance.

affaire, *f.*; excursionner; fête, *f.*; marchander; monument, *m.*; musée, *m.*; passeport, *m.*; place, *f.*; séjour, *m.*

Tour guide

Je voudrais vous demander de me rendre service. Mon oncle va bientôt visiter cette région pour la première fois et il voudrait bien sûr tout voir. Malheureusement, j'aurai très peu de temps et de plus, je connais assez mal la région. Vous qui êtes guides touristiques, pouvez-vous lui expliquer ce qu'il y a à voir dans la région? Je vous en serais très reconnaissant(e).

admirable; architecte, *m.*; architecture, *m.*; attraction, *f.*; bureau de tourisme, *m.*; cathédrale, *f.*; demander; exposition, *f.*; Hôtel de ville, *m.*; parc d'attractions, *m.*; unique

Visiting scholar

Des nouvelles merveilleuses! Vous êtes tous récipients d'une bourse pour passer un an dans un pays où l'on parle français. On exige seulement que vous ne parliez que le français pendant tout le temps que vous serez là-bas. Je sais que ceci sera difficile, donc je pense que vous devez former des groupes pour vous entre-aider. Dans ces groupes vous pouvez envisager des problèmes éventuels tels que: où vivre, comment rencontrer les gens, et comment vous inscrire à la faculté ou au lycée. Il n'y a pas de temps à perdre. Dépêchez-vous!

appartement, *m.*; change, *m.*; cours obligatoire; difficile à trouver; dortoir, *m.*; frais d'inscription, *m.*; illégal; s'inscrire; logement, *m.*; règlement, *m.*; spécialité, *f.*; transport, *m.*

Nostalgia

Nous voici enfin à la 25e réunion de la clase de 19 – – du lycée Paul Marchand. Je sais que vous êtes tous ravis de revoir vos anciens amis. Alors, vous devez avoir envie de vous parler des changements dans vos vies depuis vingt-cinq ans. Essayez de vous souvenir de comment vous étiez il y a vingt-cinq ans.

Variation (*continuez*) Il n'y a que moi qui vous connaissais tous alors et encore maintenant, donc je vais vous rappeler qui vous êtes et étiez.

basketball, *m.*; changer; couronné de succès; échec, *m.*; ensemble; entraîneur, *m.*; mémoire, *f.*; nostalgique; surprendre; tradition, *f.*

High society

Il y a une nouvelle merveilleuse pour vous. Vous êtes tous invités à une soirée de gala qui aura lieu au château de M. et Mme Charles Bienplacé de la Forêt, le couple le plus riche et le plus chic de cette ville. Mais attention! Il faut y aller non pas comme de simples étudiants, mais comme les gens riches et cultivés que vous êtes en réalité. Il y parmi vous des milliardaires, des vedettes de cinéma, des athlètes connus, des diplomates, des écrivains, des politiciens, des espions, et ainsi de suite. Un de vous est garçon de café. Pensez une minute à vos identités. Ensuite à la soirée, présentez-vous aux autres, bavardez et racontez les derniers scandales.

Variation (*continuez*) Si par hasard vous avez oublié pour le moment votre vraie identité, je vais vous la rappeler. Je vais donner à chaque personne une feuille de papier qui révèle sa propre identité.

bavardage, *m.*; élégant; ennuyeux; formel; insulte, *f.*; invitation, *f.*; porter un toast; renommée, *f.*; riche; rumeur, *f.*

Visitation

Aujourd'hui nous allons avoir quelques invités assez originaux. Comme vous le savez peut-être, j'ai des pouvoirs magiques. J'adore parler aux fantômes, surtout à ceux des gens célèbres. J'ai décidé de vous laisser choisir les personnages célèbres du passé que vous voudriez connaître. Après que je les ai emmenés ici, vous aurez l'occasion de les interviewer.

bataille, *f.*; découverte, *f.*; empire, *m.*; femme de science, *f.*; général, *m.*; homme de science, *m.*; inventer; reine, *f.*; roi, *m.*; vaincre; vainqueur, *m.*

Honored guest

On a besoin de vous tout de suite! On est sur le point de commencer le dîner qui honore le président de la Zanzanie. La Zanzanie est un pays très controversé et son président n'est pas très apprécié. Au dernier moment, tous nos dirigeants d'industries importantes ainsi que tous nos fonctionnaires ont refusé d'assister à ce repas. On vient de vous engager en tant que remplaçants. C'est-à-dire que vous devez faire semblant d'être des cadres proéminents dans nos industries, dans notre gouvernement, et dans notre armée. Tout ceci pour duper le président de la Zanzanie! Vous devez chacun faire un petit discours en l'honneur du président de la Zanzanie. Je vous donnerai vos nouvelles identités.

avare; bienveillant; brillant; dédié; esprit de commandement, *m.*; héros, *m.*; inspirateur; intrépide; prévoyance; puissant

Convention

Frères et soeurs de l'Ordre Loyal et Bienveillant du Rhinocéros—notre société secrète. Vous aurez tous le privilège d'assister à notre conférence nationale merveilleuse. Je suis certain(e) que vous tous—nouveaux membres ainsi qu'anciens membres—passerez un moment inoubliable dans cette grande ville. Pensez à des tours à jouer aux autres, à de nouveaux rites, et à de nouvelles traditions à instaurer.

ancien, *m.*; bruyant; casser; du plaisir; s'enivrer; se faire arrêter; ivre; société, *f.*; sot; tumultueux

Emergency

Quelle catastrophe! Le vieux barrage du réservoir vient de s'écrouler! Toute la région est inondée! A vous membres de l'équipe de sauvetage de vous rendre sur place immédiatement. Vous qui y êtes déjà, vous êtes coincés par les eaux fluviales. Il faut donc agir le plus vite possible.

blessé; boîtes de conserves, *f.*; chercher; civière, *f.*; dangereux; eau potable, *f.*; hors-bord, *m.*; premiers soins, *m.*; nourrir; secours, *m.*; traiter

German appendix

Treasures

Ich bin verwirrt. Heute morgen, als ich unterwegs zur Schule war, hielt mich ein Mann, der eine große Plastiktüte trug, auf. Diesen Gegenstand nahm er aus der Tüte. Er versicherte mir, daß er sehr wertvoll sei, aber da er Geld brauchte, würde er ihn mir zu nur 200,—DM verkaufen. Da ich auf ein Sonderangebot nie verzichten kann, kaufte ich ihn ihm sofort ab. Nun bin ich nicht so sicher, daß ich richtig handelte, denn ich habe keine Ahnung, was dieses Ding ist. Da ich weiß, ihr seid Antiquitätenkenner, bitte ich euch darum, mich darüber aufzuklären, und mir zu sagen, ob ich betrogen worden bin.

alt; dick; hart; kostspielig; kunstvoll; rund; schwer; viereckig; weich; zerbrechlich

Family portrait

Gestern abend war ich oben in meinem Speicher und machte zufällig eine alte staubbedeckte Truhe auf. In der Truhe fand ich dieses Foto. Es gibt keine Anmerkungen darauf, aber ich vermute, daß ich mit einigen Leuten im Lichtbild verwandt bin. Ich weiß, ihr versteht euch auf Familienforschung. Ich konnte eben nicht warten, euch das Foto zu zeigen, damit ihr mir sagen könntet, wer diese Leute waren, und was sie machten, als die Aufnahme geknipst wurde.

komisch; liebevoll; mutig; der Photograph; schön; schüchtern; schwarz und weiß; stolz, der Verbrecher

Art critic

Wie einige von euch schon wissen, war mein lieber Onkel Oskar ein Kunstsammler, der wegen der komischen und merkwürdigen Werke seiner Sammlung berühmt war. Er sagte oft, daß in jedem Werk eine Geschichte versteckt sei. Also, Onkel Oskar ist im vorigen Monat gestorben, und hat mir einige seiner Lieblingswerke hinterlassen. Das Problem ist, daß ich gar nichts von Kunst verstehe, und mir wird nicht klar, was die Gemälde bedeuten, und warum sie wertvoll sind. Da ich weiß, ihr seid begabte Kunstinterpreten und -historiker, bitte ich euch, mir die Bedeutung der darin dargestellten Geschichten zu erzählen, und ihre Wichtigkeit zu beurteilen.

dunkel; hell; der Hintergrund; der Kritiker; das Kunstwerk; malen; die Malerei; das Meisterwerk; ruhig; tief

Flute flight

Als ich letzten Sommer in einem fernen Land reiste, hörte ich eine Musik, die mir vollkommen fremd war. Ihre besonderen Eigenschaften haben mich fasziniert. Glücklicherweise konnte ich eine Tonaufnahme davon kaufen. Da ich in Eile war, hatte ich keine Zeit, mich über den Ursprung und die Bedeutung dieser Musik zu erkundigen. Ich habe aber gehört, daß die Leute in der Gegend oft durch Musik Geschichten erzählt hätten. Ihr alle seid Experten in der Musik der Welt. Daher bitte ich euch um eine Erklärung des Ursprungs dieser Musik und eine Nacherzählung ihrer Geschichte.

die Flöte; die Gitarre; die Harmonie; heiter; komponieren; laut; lebhaft; leise; musizieren; trauervoll; die Trommel

Tapestry

Heute habe ich ein außergewöhnliches Stück Stoff bei mir. Es wurde nach einem geheimen Vorgang von längst verstorbenen Webern hergestellt. Soviel ich weiß, bleibt dieses Stück als letztes übrig. Dieser Stoff ist äußerst brauchbar und hat mehrere wunderbare Eigenschaften. Es freut mich, daß ihr heute da seid. Diejenigen, die Textilienhersteller sind, werden Gelegenheit haben, sich einen Wiederherstellungsvorgang auszudenken. Diejenigen, die Textilwaren verkaufen, können eine Liste der Verwendungsmöglichkeiten aufstellen. Diejenigen, die Experten der Weltreligionen sind, können das Glaubenssystem erklären, das durch die sich wiederholenden Muster im Stoff symbolisiert wird.

dehnen; dick; elastisch; färben; nachbilden; nähen; wasserdicht; weben; weich; zerreißen

College application

Die Sekretärin des Zulassungskomitees hat gerade angerufen. Dort hat man ein außergewöhnliches Anmeldungsformular erhalten. Sie wissen nicht, was sie damit machen sollen. Sie wollen dem Bewerber gegenüber fair sein, aber sie haben nie so einen Menschen gesehen. Um das alles noch schlechter zu machen, hat jemand Kaffee auf den Antrag vergossen, und jetzt ist viel davon unlesbar. Da die Zeit zu knapp ist, Kontakt mit dem Bewerber aufzunehmen, braucht das Zulassungskomitee eure Hilfe. Als Fachleute anderer Kulturen bittet sie euch um eine Erklärung davon, was der Bewerber wohl geschrieben hat. Sie müssen wissen, wer er/sie ist, und, warum er/sie glaubt, daß er/sie zugelassen werden sollte. Hier ist das Foto, das dem Anmeldungsformular angeheftet war.

der Athlet; die Flossen; das Geweih; die Hufe; intuitiv; der Musiker; mysteriös; der Pfeil und der Bogen; der Ringer; der Tänzer

Character sketch

Der Redakteur dieser Bücher hat entschlossen, daß die nächste Ausgabe Abbildungen enthalten muß. Dieser Redakteur glaubt, Bilder der Hauptcharaktere würden helfen, mehr Bücher zu verkaufen. Da ihr bekannte Künstler seid, wurdet ihr beauftragt, die Illustrationen zu zeichnen. Erinnert euch daran, daß euer Werk den Text genau abbilden soll.

Omelet

Wir haben ein Problem. Der Computer hat sich verrechnet. Morgen zu dieser Zeit werden drei Millionen Eier ins Klassenzimmer geliefert. Es wäre furchtbar verschwenderisch, die Eier verderben zu lassen. Da ihr Lebensmittelverwendungs- und Vertriebsexperten seid, sollt ihr euch möglichst viele Verwendungs- und Vertriebsmöglichkeiten ausdenken.

ausrollen; braten; dehydrieren; faul; kochen; die Rühreier; das Spiegelei; teilen; das Toastbrot; verzieren

Flim-flam

Ich bin pleite. Ich komme mit meinem Lehrergehalt nicht zurecht. Ihr wißt, wie wenig Lehrer bezahlt bekommen. Ich will über Nacht reich werden. Da ich weiß, ihr seid Geldanschaffungsspezialisten, aber nicht, sagen wir mal, durchaus ehrlich, dachte ich, daß ihr mir vorschlagen könntet, auf welche Art und Weise ich möglichst schnell viel Geld erwerben könnte. Betrügen des breiten Publikums ist mir recht, aber seid doch bitte vorsichtig. Ich will nicht im Gefängnis landen!

der Betrüger; das Darlehen; die Erfindung; gefälscht; das Kostüm; liefern; die Nachahmung; die Uniform; versprechen; vormachen

Flagging

Juchhe! Lang lebe die Republik Bartonia! Bartonia hat gerade ihre Unabhängigkeit erhalten. Es wird auf der Straße getanzt! Es gibt allerdings ein Problem. Bartonias Gründer haben sich über eine Fahne für den neuen Staat nicht einigen können. Der Botschafter bittet euch—geschickte Fahnenhersteller—um einen Fahnenentwurf. Die Farben und Muster, die ihr wählt, sollten von großer Bedeutung für Bartonias Staatsbürger sein. Wenn ihr noch Zeit habt, könnt ihr auch einen Fahneneid schreiben.

achtseitig; der Adler; das Dreieck; der Pfeil; rechteckig; das Schild; schwenken; der Stern; das Sternbild; die Streifen

Perfect person

Es stört mich sehr, daß jeder einzelne Mensch, den ich kennenlerne, unvollkommen ist. Ich bin wirklich müde damit. Jeder, den ich kenne, hat Mängel, Schwächen, schlechte Gewohnheiten und andere Unvollkommenheiten. Als Biologen bitte ich euch, den perfekten Menschen zu entwerfen.

freigiebig; gut gebaut; der Humor; liebenswürdig; reich; reif; schöpferisch; selbstbewußt; tapfer; weise; wohlwollend; zuversichtlich

Recycle

Es gibt einfach zuviel Verschwendung. Der örtliche Müllabladeplatz ist mit Dingen überhäuft, die nochmals benutzt werden könnten. Als Wiederverwertungsexperten hat der Bürgermeister euch gebeten, Listen neuer Verwendungsmöglichkeiten für gebrauchte Gegenstände aufzustellen.

abgenutzt; anpassen; nützlich; nutzlos; streichen; die Verzierung; wiederaufbauen; wiederverwenden; wiegen; zurechtmachen

Dinner party

Ich hoffe, du hast nicht vergessen, daß sechs Leute morgen abend zum Abendessen zu dir kommen. Da die Zeit knapp wird, wäre es sehr viel leichter, wenn du das Menü aufgrund der Angebote eines Lebensmittelgeschäfts auswählen könntest. Glücklicherweise sind die Anzeigen auf deutsch. Anhand der angezeigten Information sollst du eine köstliche Mahlzeit planen. Du darfst soviel ausgeben wie du willst, aber trag die Unkosten ein!

backen; braten; die Flasche; frisch; der Kuchen; die Nachspeise; die Nahrung; sauer

Vacation

Ich bin erschöpft! Diese Klasse hat mich ermüdet. Ich muß in den Urlaub, aber ich bin so müde, daß mir die Energie fehlt, um dafür zu planen. Da ihr geschickte, erfahrene Reisende seid, bitte ich euch darum, mir den Urlaub zu planen. Es ist mir egal, wieviel er kostet.

sich ausruhen; Autostop machen; der Blick; die Bräune; gelassen; geschäftig; der Kurort; die Küste; photographieren; zelten

Animal house

Ich habe gerade einen Anruf vom Direktor des örtlichen Zoos bekommen. Er sagte mir, daß er sich Sorgen mache, weil der Zoobesuch geringer sei als je zuvor. Es scheint, das Publikum hat das Interesse an die Tiere verloren. Er bittet euch als Biologen um die Erfindung eines neuen, interessanteren Tieres. Ihm wäre geholfen, wenn ihr dieses Tier zusammen mit seiner Heimat, seinem Essen, seiner Gestalt und anderen Besonderheiten beschreiben könntet.

der Fleischfresser; das Geweih; der Hals; der Huf; die Mähne; der Pflanzenfresser; die Pfote; der Rüssel; der Schwanz; der Stoßzahn

Student center

Ich habe eine aufregende Nachricht. Die Universitätsverwaltung hat euch ausgewählt, ein neues Gebäude für das Studentenzentrum zu entwerfen. Als Architekten sollt ihr das vollkommenste und modernste Gebäude dieser Art planen. Gebt soviel Geld aus wie ihr wollt, und schafft den Studenten ein Gebäude, das sie benutzen und genießen werden.

die Garderobe; der Gesellschaftsraum; der Hörsaal; Karten spielen; plaudern; das Schließfach; das Schwimmbad; spielen; die Turnhalle; der Versammlungssaal; der Wettkampf

House party

Der Bürgermeister braucht eure Hilfe. Ein reicher Junggeselle ist gestorben und hat der Stadt sein riesiges achtzehn-Zimmer-Haus hinterlassen. Als Architekten bittet der Bürgermeister euch um eine Liste der Verwendungsmöglichkeiten für das Haus und auch um eine ausführliche Beschreibung eures Lieblingsplans.

das Büro, das Eßzimmer; der Flur; das Geschäft; die Herberge; der Kindergarten; das Klassenzimmer; die Klinik; die Küche; das Theater

Hobby town

Mir ist's langweilig. Meine alten Hobbys interessieren mich nicht mehr. Ich kann mir nichts einfallen lassen, wie ich meine Freizeit verbringen sollte. Als Experten auf dem Gebiet der Unterhaltung bitte ich euch, mir beim Planen meiner Freizeit zu helfen. Ihr sollt eine Liste von Tätigkeiten aufstellen, die ich wirklich genießen werde, und ein neues Hobby erfinden, das mich nicht langweilen wird.

die Antiquitäten; die Briefmarken; das Modell; organisieren; die Rakete; reparieren; sammeln; spannend; tropische Fische; wiederaufbauen

Chef

Herzlichen Glückwunsch! Die Akademie der Kochkünste hat euch als Meisterköche ausgewählt, das Menü zum Promovierungsbankett vorzubereiten. Die Wahl der Zutaten ist unbegrenzt. Ihr dürft irgendetwas planen, aber was ihr serviert, muß dem Auge gefallen und sehr lecker sein. Habt keine Angst vor dem Erfinden neuer Gerichte!

braten; das Eis; das Fleisch; das Gemüse; grillen; das Kotelett; der Reis; schlagen; die Schlagsahne; schmieren; schwenken; die Soße; die Torte

Floating

Es freut mich, mitteilen zu können, daß diese Klasse ausgewählt worden ist, einen Festwagen für den Stiftergedenktag zu entwerfen. Nach Angaben des Paradeausschusses dürft ihr planen, soviel auszugeben wie ihr wollt. Die Auswahl der zu verwendenden Materialien steht euch frei. Die Festwagen werden ihrer Kreativität und Schönheit nach von einer Gruppe berühmter Persönlichkeiten bewertet werden. Ihr müßt euren Festwagen beschreiben und auch einen Bauplan zeichnen.

bauen; die Fahne; das Geländer; der Motor; rechteckig; rund; schräg; der Thron; die Treppe; der Turm

Toyland

Mein bester Freund Richard braucht euren Rat. Seine kleinen Nichten und Neffen kommen zum Besuch. Richard ist aber Junggeselle. Er besitzt überhaupt keine Spielzeuge. Er möchte sich einige Spielzeuge verschaffen, mit denen die Kinder spielen können, aber er kann sich nicht viel leisten und hat keine Ahnung, was Kinder mögen. Er bittet euch als Erziehungsberater, ihm eine Liste von amüsanten, sicheren aber auch billigen Spielzeugen und Spielen aufzustellen. Mindestens eins davon soll eure eigene Erfindung sein.

austauschen; der Faden; hüpfen; die Klötze; die Kugel; der Pfahl; der Plattenspieler; die Schachtel; der Spielkamerad; springen; sich verstecken

Snake oil

Heutzutage ist es schwer, Arzt zu sein. Es ist sehr frustrierend. Nach so vielen Jahren ärztlicher Entdeckungen gibt es immer noch zu viele Krankheiten, die die Ärzte nicht heilen können. Sie brauchen ein neues Wunderarzneimittel. Als Fachleute der Chemie liegt es an euch, ein neues Arzneimittel zu entwickeln, das allerlei Krankheiten heilen wird.

das Antibiotikum; der Blutdruck; die Dosis; das Fieber; flüssig; juckend; der Kreislauf; die Pillen; die Reizung; das Rezept; die Spritze

Planning board

Die Verhältnisse in Berghausen sind eine Schande. Jahre schlechter Verwaltung des Bürgermeisters und Stadtrats haben eine heruntergekommene, marode Stadt zur Folge. Glücklicherweise ist eine neue Reformverwaltung gerade ins Amt getreten, und ihr werdet beim Planungsausschuß mitarbeiten. Mehrere wichtige Projekte müssen gleich erledigt werden. Unter anderen sind eine stadtweite Reinigung, ein Lärmreduzierungsprogramm und der Aufbau eines neuen U-Bahnsystems geplant. Die Entwürfe sollen erfinderisch und originell sein. Machen wir aus Berghausen eine vorbildliche Stadt!

der Abfall; aufbauen; der Bahnhof; die Klimaanlage; der Müll; räumen; schalldicht; städtisch; die U-Bahn; die Verordnung

Shipwreck

Ich hatte recht. Ich wollte nach Tahiti fliegen, aber ihr habt darauf bestanden, mit dem Schiff zu fahren. Während eines furchtbaren pazifischen Sturmes versank das Schiff. Wir haben alle Glück, überhaupt am Leben zu sein. Irgendwie haben wir's geschafft, eine Insel zu erreichen. Das Klima ist angenehm, und es gibt viel Vegetation. Keine anderen Leute sind auf der Insel. Alles, was wir haben, sind die Kleider, die wir tragen, Streichhölzer, Messer, Draht und einige Arzneimittel. Wir müssen für uns selbst sorgen. Wir brauchen einen Plan. Es könnte lange dauern, bis die Hilfe ankommt.

fischen; die Hütte; jagen; die Kleidung; die Liegematte; das Obdach; primitiv; sammeln; weben

Zodiac

Es ist wieder passiert. Ein Horoskop war völlig falsch. Nicht nur das—immer mehr Leute behaupten, daß ihre Persönlichkeiten den traditionellen Sternzeichen, wie zum Beispiel dem Widder und dem Löwen, nicht entsprechen. Da ihr gute Astrologen seid, könnt ihr helfen. Ihr habt die nötigen Kenntnisse, um neue Sternzeichen zu identifizieren und die charakteristischen Eigenschaften derjenigen Personen zu beschreiben, die unter diesen Zeichen geboren wurden.

faul; fleißig; freundlich; geschickt; mütterlich; ruhelos; schöpferisch; selbstbewußt; sorglos; zynisch

Tribal council

Ich habe eine furchtbare Nachricht. Infolge eines Erlasses der Regierung müßt ihr das Landesgebiet, auf dem eure Sippenschaft seit Generationen wohnt, verlassen und in eine andere Gegend umziehen. Da ihr die Sippen-ältesten seid, müßt ihr euch auf eine tiefgründige Änderung des sippen-schaftlichen Lebensstils vorbereiten. Dort wird es begrenzte Hilfsquellen geben. Wenn die Sachen richtig verwaltet werden, wird die Sippenschaft gedeihen. Wenn nicht, geht sie zugrunde. Die Pläne, die ihr nun macht, werden auf künftige Generationen wirken.

der Bauernhof; das Eigentum; die Grenze; die Industrie; die Konkurrenz; das Lager; die Regierung; das Rindvieh; die Steuer; zustimmen

Quick sale

Ich habe eine dringende Nachricht. Die Studiengebühren sind erhöht worden. Um Finanzierungsschwierigkeiten zu vermeiden, hat die Verwaltung beschlossen, daß Studenten den Preisunterschied sofort zu bezahlen haben. Um das Geld aufzubringen, müßt ihr euren Klassenkameraden etwas verkaufen, das ihr im Moment bei euch habt. Schreibt Anzeigen, die zum Ankauf anreizen.

die Armbanduhr; automatisch; das Bargeld; billig; der Gelegenheitskauf; das Lineal; der Photoapparat; der Preis; der Ring; die Tüte

Soft soap

Wir haben Glück! Die Firma XYZ Waschmittel hat gerade unser Werbe-büro FEE, FIE, FOE, FUM zur Mitarbeit engagiert. Diese Firma besteht darauf, daß ihre Produkte besser und stärker sind als irgendetwas, was jetzt auf dem Markt ist. Sie sind einfach außerordentlich leistungsfähig. Als die besten Inseratenverfasser habt ihr die Aufgabe, Inserate zu schreiben, die viele neue Kunden anziehen werden.

die Bleiche; dreckig; fleckenlos; makellos; das Reinigungsmittel; der Scheuerlappen; schmuddelig; der Schwamm; die Wäsche; die Waschmaschine

Used car

Ich habe ein Problem. Schon seit Monaten versuche ich, meinen Wagen loszuwerden, aber keiner will ihn kaufen. Er fährt gut, und der Preis ist auch sehr günstig. Leute sagen mir aber wiederholt, er sei zu merkwürdig, zu seltsam und zu andersartig. Ihr seid meine letzte Hoffnung. Ich bitte euch als erfahrene Werbeagenten, eine Anzeige zu verfassen, die den Verkauf meines Autos garantieren wird.

Ach, ich habe vergessen, ein Foto des Autos mitzubringen, aber sicher könnt ihr euch vorstellen, wie mein außergewöhnliches Auto aussieht. Ihr möchtet vielleicht sogar ein Bild davon zeichnen.

die Bremse; die Geschwindigkeit; die Haube; die Heizung; die Hupe; das Kabriolett; Kilometer pro Stunde; die Klimaanlage; der Motor; der Reifen; die Windschutz-scheibe

Alma mater

Unsere beliebte Universität ist in ernster Not. Da so wenige neue Studenten nächstes Jahr auf die Uni kommen werden, müssen viele Studiengänge gestrichen werden. Wenn das Problem einige Jahre lang so weitergeht, muß die gesamte Uni geschlossen werden. Nur ihr könnt helfen. Da ihr eure Uni liebt und ihre besonderen Werte kennt, seid ihr am geeignetesten, Inserate zu schreiben, die neue Studenten anziehen und fortgegangene Kommilitonen zur Rückkehr über-zeugen werden.

beruflich; führend; intensiv; der Lehrplan; praktisch; die Qualität; schöpferisch; spezialisiert; technisch

Campaign

Meiner Meinung nach sind alle Kandidaten für die nächste Wahl unfähig. Es gibt überhaupt keine angesehenen Kandidaten mehr. Als Antwort darauf habe ich euch die Nominierung beliebiger Persönlichkeiten aus der Gegenwart bzw. Vergangenheit arrangiert, die für dieses wichtige Amt kandidieren können. Die Leute, die ihr nominiert, müssen nicht aus diesem Land kommen, und sie brauchen nicht mehr am Leben zu sein. Sie müssen nicht einmal existiert haben.

Sie dürfen sehr außergewöhnlich sein. Ihr müßt einen Kandidaten aussuchen. Dann erfindet Wahlsprüche und politische Literatur, die diesen Kandidaten unterstützen.

sich um ein Amt bewerben; ehrfurchtsvoll; ehrlich; gewissenhaft; konservativ; der Liberale; der Linksradikale; das Parteiprogramm; der Rechte; sparsam; tapfer; vertrauenswürdig

Tourist office

Es freut mich sehr, Sie als Vertreter der Fremdenverkehrsministerien Ihrer Länder zur Uno-Tagung, die dem Jahr des Touristen zu Ehren stattfindet, begrüßen zu können. Wie Sie wissen, bedrohen steigende Reisekosten die Zukunft des Fremdenverkehrs und damit die Wirtschaft Ihrer Länder. Ihre Aufgabe während der Tagung besteht darin, neue und überzeugende Darstellungen Ihrer Länder zu formulieren, die potentielle Touristen anziehen werden.

Die Vertreter aus Reichlandien, Mittellandien und Armlandien werden in voneinander getrennten Gruppen arbeiten, um ihre Materialien vorzubereiten. Später kommen wir nochmals zusammen und stellen unsere Ideen vor der gesamten Gruppe auf die Probe.

altmodisch; bergig; bildhaft; das Denkmal; entspannend; exklusiv; geschichtlich; das Kasino; der Kurort; malerisch; reizend; unberührt; weltbürgerlich

Mansion

Ich kann es einfach nicht verstehen. Diese wunderschönen Häuser sind schon seit Monaten auf dem Markt, aber kein Mensch will sie kaufen. Die Grundstücksmakler sind sehr frustriert. Sie bitten euch als erfahrene Grundstücksmakler, Inserate zu schreiben, die Käufern imponieren werden. Sollten die Häuser verkauft werden, werdet ihr eine große Provision bekommen.

ausziehen; einziehen; erstklassig; die Garage; der Gemüsegarten; geräumig; die Hypothek; luxuriös; die Nachbarschaft; der Patio; das Schwimmbad; der Tennisplatz

Air waves

Die Inhaber des Radiosenders B3 machen sich große Sorgen. Es gibt weniger Zuhörer als je zuvor. Bleibt das Publikum länger aus, wird er bald schließen müssen. Nur ihr als Fachberater könnt den Radiosender retten. Eure Aufgabe ist es, Werbespots für den Rundfunk zu schreiben, die neue Zuhörer anziehen werden. Ihr dürft euch Spiele und Wettbewerbe einfallen lassen, die im Rundfunk gespielt werden können. Neue Programme dürft ihr auch vorschlagen. Retten wir B3!

der Ansager; die Anzeigetafel; die Frequenz; das Liedchen; die Nachrichten; der Sportberichterstatter; verbessert; der Wettbewerb; das Wettrennen

Last rites

Ich habe eine sehr traurige Nachricht. Mehrere international bekannte Personen sind plötzlich gestorben. Unter anderen sind der ehrenwerte Alphonsus Muggeridge, ehemaliger Botschafter der Republik Wellingtonien in den Vereinigten Staaten von Amerika, Max „Die Fliege" Jones, berüchtigter Mörder, Juwelendieb und Mitglied der Uptown-Verbrecherbande, und die Dame Edith Grellton, Solistin bei der Westlichen Oper. Diese Todesereignisse sollen jedoch nicht unbemerkt vergehen. Als experte Journalisten habt ihr die Ehre, die Todesanzeigen für diese wichtigen Menschen zu verfassen.

das Attentat; die Beerdigung; gefürchtet; der Herzinfarkt; eine lange Krankheit; religiös; die Schenkung; verehrt; der/die Verstorbene

Dead language

Ich habe gerade eine beunruhigende Nachricht erhalten. Kursanmeldungen für Hondari—die Sprache in Hondaristan—lassen drastisch nach. Studenten schreiben sich für diese früher beliebte Sprache nicht mehr ein. Die Universitätsverwaltung droht, das Fach Hondari zu streichen. Als Experten in vielen Sprachen und ernsthafte Studenten des Fremdsprachstudiums werdet ihr vom Vorsitzenden der Fremdsprachenabteilung dringend gebeten, der Verwaltung einen Brief zu schreiben, in dem ihr erklärt, warum Hondari unterrichtet werden sollte. Schlagt auch vor, wie man neue Studenten zum Fach heranziehen kann!

der Diplomat; die Diplomatie; der Export; der Fremdenverkehr; der Import; die Kultur; die Literatur; der Reiseverkehr; der/die Verbündete; der Vertrag; die Zivilisation

Taxi driver

Nach einem anstrengenden siebenstündigen Flug kommst du endlich in Wallen, der Hauptstadt von Contursien, an. Glüklicherweise findest du ein Taxi. Du bist ein bißchen nervös, denn du sprichst kein Wort Contursi, und der

Taxifahrer kennt kein Wort deiner Muttersprache. Kurz darauf erfährst du jedoch, daß der Fahrer die gleiche Sprache studiert hat und genaussoviel davon kann wie du. Vom Flughafen zum Stadtzentrum dauert es eine Zeitlang. Ihr werdet also genügend Zeit haben, euch kennenzulernen.

bereisen; bleiben; das Denkmal; das Fest; der Gelegenheitskauf; handeln; das Museum; der Paß; der Platz

Tour guide

Ich muß euch um einen Gefallen bitten. Mein Onkel kommt zum Besuch. Er ist zum ersten Mal da, und er will alle Sehenswürdigkeiten besichtigen. Nächste Woche habe ich sehr wenig Zeit. Außerdem kenne ich mich nicht besonders gut in der Gegend aus. Da ihr erfahrene Fremdenführer seid, könnt ihr meinem Onkel die hiesigen Sehenswürdigkeiten vorstellen. Ich wäre euch sehr dankbar dafür.

der Architekt; die Architektur; die Ausstellung; der Dom; einzigartig; sich erkundigen; das Rathaus; die Sehenswürdigkeit; der Vergnügungspark; das Verkehrsamt; vortrefflich

Visiting scholar

Ich habe eine wunderbare Nachricht! Ihr habt Stipendien bekommen, um ein Jahr in einem deutschsprachigen Land zu verbringen. Die einzige Bedingung besteht darin, daß ihr während des Aufenthalts nur Deutsch sprecht. Da das euch schwerfallen wird, wäre es eine gute Idee, Arbeitsgruppen zu bilden. Fangt schon vor der Abfahrt zu üben an! In den Gruppen könnt ihr diskutieren, wie man mit solchen Problemen wie Wohnungssuche, Inlandsreisen, Essen, Bekanntschaften und Anmeldung an einer Universität fertig wird. Man soll keine Zeit verlieren. Ihr sollt sofort anfangen.

das Haupfach; illegal; immatrikulieren; die Ordnung; das Pflichtfach; schwer zu finden; das Studentenheim; das Verkehrsmittel; der Wechselkurs; die Wohnung

Nostalgia

Glücklicherweise seid ihr alle zum 25. Wiedertreffen des Jahrgangs 19 – – des Jasmin-Gymnasiums eingeladen worden. Da ihr alle Jahrgang 19 – – seid, bin ich sicher, ihr werdet euch aufs Wiedersehen mit alten Freunden und auf Plaudereien über die persönlichen Veränderungen der letzten 25 Jahre freuen. Versucht euch ans Geschwätz aus den guten alten Zeiten am Jasmin-Gymnasium zu erinnern!

Variation (*Setzen Sie fort!*) Da ich die einzige Person bin, die euch schon seit langem kennt, werde ich euch an eure derzeitigen Identitäten erinnern. (Wählen Sie Studenten aus, die die Rollen des besten Athleten, des Klassenführers, des Schüchternen, des Durchschnittsschülers, des Schreiers, des Protestierenden, usw. spielen sollen.)

sich ändern; erfolgreich; die Erinnerung; das Korbballspiel; sehnsüchtig; die Tradition; der Trainer; überraschen; der Versager; zusammen

High society

Ihr seid zum Gala Ball im Patrizierhaus der Familie Rutherford Upstreet eingeladen worden. Die Upstreets sind die reichsten und vornehmsten Bürger dieser Stadt. Jeder von euch wird dem Ball beiwohnen, aber nicht wie ihr jetzt ins Klassenzimmer kommt, sondern wie die vornehmen Persönlichkeiten, die ihr meines Erachtens wirklich seid. Mehrere von euch sind Millionäre, andere sind Filmstars, Profi-Athleten, Figuren der Unterwelt, Schriftsteller, Diplomaten, Generäle, Botschafter, Politiker und Playboys. Einer von euch ist Kellner. Denkt einen Augenblick über eure wahre Identität nach! Dann auf der Party stellt euch den Anderen vor, plaudert und diskutiert über die jüngsten Skandale!

Variation (*Setzen Sie fort!*) Falls ihr eure wahren Rollen momentan vergessen habt, werde ich euch daran erinnern. Ich gebe jedem von euch einen Zettel, auf dem eure wirkliche Identität steht.

die Blamage; die Einladung; elegant; formell; das Gerücht; der Klatsch; langweilig; reich; der Ruhm; trinken auf

Visitation

Heute werden wir einige ziemlich außergewöhnliche Gäste haben. Wie einige von euch wissen, habe ich die Fähigkeit zu zaubern. Ich rede nämlich gern mit Gespenstern, besonders mit den Gespenstern berühmter Menschen. Ich habe die Entscheidung getroffen, euch zu erlauben, beliebte Persönlichkeiten aus der Vergangenheit auszuwählen. Als Historiker werdet ihr Gelegenheit haben, sie zu interviewen, nachdem ich sie heraufbeschwöre.

besiegen; die Entdeckung; erfinden; erobern; der General; der König; die Königin; das Reich; die Schlacht; der Sieger; der Wissenschaftler

Honored guest

Eure Hilfe wird sofort benötigt. In wenigen Minuten beginnt das Staatsessen, das zu Ehren des Präsidenten von Zanzanien gegeben wird. Zanzanien ist ein sehr kontroverses Land, und sein Präsident ist höchst unbeliebt. Zanzanien ist jedoch unserem Land Bartonien sehr wichtig. Im letzten Moment haben alle führenden Geschäftsleute und Regierungsbeamten abgelehnt, dem Essen beizuwohnen. Ihr seid angestellt worden, um sie zu ersetzen. Um den Präsidenten täuschen zu können, müßt ihr als führende Geschäftsleute und Regierungsmitglieder bzw. Offiziere auftreten. Jeder von euch muß eine kurze Rede halten oder einen Trinkspruch auf den Präsidenten sagen. Ich werde eure neuen Rollen an euch verteilen.

begeistert; die Führung; furchtlos; gierig; glänzend; der Held; imponierend; kräftig; die Voraussicht; wohltätig; zugeneigt

Convention

Brüder und Schwestern der höchst geheimen Gesellschaft des Loyalen und Wohlwollenden Nashornordens! Ihr werdet die Ehre haben, unserer Nationaltagung beizuwohnen. Ich bin sicher, daß sowohl alte als auch neue Mitglieder sich in der Großstadt sehr vergnügen werden. Ich bin auch sicher, ihr werdet euch neue Streiche sowie neue Rituale und Traditionen ausdenken.

älteres Mitglied; sich betrinken; betrunken; brechen; geräuschvoll; läppisch; lärmend; Spaß; der Verein; verhaftet

Emergency

Es ist ein schweres Unglück geschehen. Die alte Talsperre am Reservoir ist gebrochen und das ganze Gebiet ist überschwemmt. Diejenigen von euch, die Mitglieder der Rettungsmannschaft sind, müssen sofort zum Unglücksort hingehen. Andere von euch sind vom Hochwasser überrascht worden. Meistern wir die Lage so bald wie möglich.

behandeln; Erste Hilfe; füttern; gefährlich; die Hilfe; die Konservendosen; das Motorboot; suchen; die Tragbahre; das Trinkwasser; verletzt